SECRETS

T.J. ROHLEDER
The Blue Jeans Millionaire

Copyright © MMXIII Direct Response Network.

All Rights Reserved. No part of this book may be used or reproduced in any manner whatsoever without the written permission of the Publisher. Printed in the United States of America. For information address:

Direct Response Network
PO Box 198
Goessel, Kansas 67053-0198

FIRST EDITION

ISBN 1-933356-67-7

INTRODUCTION

The famous billionaire Aristotle Onassis once said, "The secret to business is to know something that none of your competitors knows." He used that mantra to build his fortune. As soon as I read his quote, I began to use it, too.

The secrets you are about to read are among the best I've used to generate tens of millions of dollars for myself and my clients. Now you can use them to build your fortune. There's nothing complicated about any of these ideas, however, they really are secrets, because most entrepreneurs and businesspeople don't know or are not using them to make more money.

For best results, study these secrets and memorize your favorite ones. Then consider how to use them to make all the money you want, need, and deserve.

And speaking of money, if you have ever wanted the perfect way to stay home and make huge sums of money, then check out my free book offer at **www.PTIW.com/freebook**. My 30-page book is yours at no cost. It's called "Get Paid Each Time Our Phone Rings!" This book tells you about our complete business opportunity that contains the best of everything I've used to generate my fortune. It shows you how I've taken my greatest secrets and built them around an amazing company from Malaysia that has already paid out over $104 million in their first six years. My staff and I are convinced that this company will ultimately pay out over one billion dollars in commissions to folks like you and me. My small book tells you how this has the potential power to pay you as much as $100,000 to $250,000 a year or more in your spare time. Best of all, we will be your joint venture partners and do some or even all of the hard work!

So if you've ever wanted the ultimate way to make huge sums of money in your spare time, please let me ship you my free book. Just go to **www.PTIW.com/freebook**. There's no cost and no obligation to purchase anything. Just fill out the simple form and I will rush it to you by first-class mail. Please do this today. I'll send you my book and show you how this can make you more money part time than most people make working full time.

MY FAVORITE SECRETS

"The 3 Ways to Build a Business" on page 1

"The Power of the Hand" on page 7

"The Safest Way to Make Money" on page 10

"The Magic Pill" on page 11

"The 4 Steps to Create Your Own Money Machine" on page 15

"How to Quickly Make More Money" on page 20

"The 4 Laws of Success" on page 24

"Marketing in Two Words" on page 28

"The Power of Exclusivity and How It Can Make You Rich" on page 32

"How Much Should You Pay Your Employees? Just Look..." on page 33

"What Most People Secretly Want and Will Never Tell You" on page 38

"The 3 Huge Mistakes Almost All Marketers are Making" on page 41

"How to Use the Secret of Gold Mining to Get Super Rich" on page 41

"The Chinese Torture Method of Marketing" on page 43

"The 6 Secrets to Instantly Increase Your Sales and Profits" on page 46

"Your Meal Ticket for Life" on page 47

"How to Get Rich by Giving Away Something for Free" on page 49

"The 3-Minute Rule of Marketing" on page 52

"The 5 Reasons Why the Right Stories Can Make You a Ton of Money" on page 52

"How to Get the Best Prospective Buyers to Chase You" on page 53

Joe Karbo's "Greatest Wealth Making Secret" on page 55

"Database Marketing in 3 Words" on page 56

"What Some Folks Would Secretly Kill Can Make You a Fortune" on page 58

"Your #1 Secret for Making All the Money You Want in Good Times or Bad" on page 59

"Why Manipulation is Good" on page 61

Robert J. Ringer's "3 Simple Money Making Rules on page 63

"A Great Wealth Making Idea from a French Revolutionary" on page 65

"The Secret of Self Promotion" on page 67

"How to Generate Your Fortune with Niche Marketing" on page 67

"Your Greatest Investment Towards Future Profits" on page 68

"Game Theory for Marketers" on page 72

"The Secret Behind Viagra and How It Can Make You a Fortune" on page 75

"Be Thankful for Your Burdens" on page 76

Bill Glazer's "Marketing Formula" on page 78

"The Game of Business and How to Play to Win!" on page 79

"The Rambo Types are the First to Go" on page 82

"The Wealth Making Secret of the Carrot and the Stick" on page 84

"The Scam of Lifetime Customer Value" on page 86

Claude Hopkin's "Greatest Secret" on page 88

"How Anger, Greed, Lust, Fear, Envy, and Even Hate Will Make You More Money" on page 91

"The #1 Secret of Success That Nobody Else Will Tell You" on page 93

"An Amazing Secret from the Mentally Insane" on page 96

"What About Love and Money?" on page 97

Donald Trump's "Greatest Business Secret" on page 97

"The 4 Secrets of Educational Marketing" on page 98

"The Killer Disease of the 21st Century" on page 99

"The Ultimate Get Rich Secret from Hollywood" on page 101

"The Only Way to Think About Advertising" on page 102

"How to Know When You've Found the Perfect Business" on page 103

"The Wealth Making Secret of the Lion King" on page 105

"The Man Who Made Tens of Millions of Dollars After Getting Rejected 144 Times" on page 107

"Why Time Management is a Terrible Idea" on page 107

"The 5 Secret Advertising Strategies That Almost Nobody Knows" on page 110

"The Simple and Easy Way to Get Extraordinary Results" on page 113

"The 3 Ways to Create Your Own Marketing System" on page 114

"Why Even the Best Consultants are Dangerous for Your Business" on page 118

Direct-Response Marketing is a personal medium:

- Write and speak <u>to</u> <u>only</u> <u>one</u> <u>person</u>.
- The art is to make the person you are communicating with seem special.
- The more you can make them feel you are <u>only</u> <u>speaking</u> <u>to</u> <u>them</u> — the better.

W.I.I.F.M.

Strive to answer the question:

"What's in it for me?"

Use <u>plain</u> — <u>direct</u> — <u>simple</u> — and FORCEFUL writing that goes <u>straight</u> to the emotions of your reader.

Work ON it — not IN it.

Be the architect of your business — <u>not</u> the worker or foreman. Definition: The architect designs the building — and sees to it that his plans are followed by the builders. The same is true in business. We must design successful marketing systems — and then monitor them closely.

There are only 3 ways to build a business:

1. Get more customers.
2. Sell more high-ticket items — for bigger profits.
3. Sell more often to your customers!

Almost all million-dollar marketing ideas are transferable from one business to another.

→ **FREE 30-Page Book at: www.PTIW.com/FreeBook**

Think in concepts.

See what others can't see — or overlook.

Emergency money-making generator...

When times get hard...

When business gets slow...

When you need cash-flow to feed the monster...

<u>All</u> <u>you</u> <u>do</u> <u>is</u>:

    a. Go to your best customers...

    b. Make them an irresistible offer they can't refuse!

    c. Have a special sale that will blow them away!

Do this and they'll stand in line with money in hand!

MASTERY

You do not become a MASTER by learning how to do 4,000 things... You become a MASTER by doing 12 important things 4,000 times!

We use hype and powerful promises for one reason:

<u>To cut through the clutter</u> of the thousands of advertising messages that are begging for our prospects and customers attention every single day.

- ❖ People are tuned out.
- ❖ They have created a tremendous resistance against ALL sales pitches.
- ❖ You have to do something dramatic to wake them up!
- ❖ You have to break through their zombie-like fog before you can pitch them.

The only way to do this is to be as dramatic as possible.

FREE 30-Page Book "Get Paid Every Time Our Phone Rings!" →

The best ideas are always an expansion and combination of previous ideas that worked.

Think on paper!

The very act of putting your ideas on paper forces you to think!

Your intimate understanding of your market and core business is the #1 ingredient for riches.

The more you know about the customer…

a. What they have bought before — or are buying now.

b. Their problems, frustration, pain, hopes, and dreams.

c. And how your product — service — company can offer them a solution to "B" — the more effective you can be at selling them.

Knowing MORE about your customer lets you MAXIMIZE the up-sell.

5 Elements Of Every Super-Successful Direct-Response Message:

1. Meaningful specifics — <u>not</u> vague generalities.
2. A promise.
3. An offer or offers.
4. Precise commands — *"Here's what I want you to do now."*
5. An extra reason to act immediately.

— *Dan Kennedy*

→ *Shipped to You for No Cost or Obligation! Go to: www.PTIW.com/FreeBook*

$ $ $ $ $

Customers in all markets want someone to do <u>everything</u> for them.

$ $ $ $ $

You must sell people the things they want — <u>NOT</u> the things you want to sell them!

* *It's all about them, not you.*

$ $ $ $ $

"Good Marketing Is A Combination Of Fishing And Chess!"

Eric Bechtold

All great fishermen know that the true secret to catching the big ones is:

1. Use the right bait.
2. Think like the fish!
3. <u>Never</u> reveal the hook.

All fishermen for sales and profits should pay attention!!

Focus on your strengths and make sure you have enough reliable people and systems in place to cover your weaknesses.

Blur the lines between your work and play.

FREE 30-Page Book "Get Paid Every Time Our Phone Rings!" →

OPERATION MONEY SUCK:

Invest <u>all</u> of your time, energy, and focus on all the various ways and means of sucking the maximum amount of money from your market.

99% of the focus should be on increasing your sales and profits. This is the life-blood of your business.

No business ever went under for having too many sales and profits!

STOP wasting your precious time, money, and energy on deadbeat prospects.

1. Do all you can to attract the very best prospects from all the rest.
2. As a general rule, those who have <u>recently</u> spent the most money or who re-buy from you on a regular basis are your <u>very</u> best prospects.
3. Develop new products and services that are as closely matched as possible to what they already bought from you.
4. Try to move your larger prospect group up the ladder — while spending the majority of your time and money on the smaller group of the highest qualified prospects.
5. Think of your entire base of customers and prospects as a triangle with the smaller group of the best buyers at the small tip on top. Can you see it? Good! Go ahead and draw it out. Then think about this: Your #1 strategy is to do all you can to increase the size and quality of the people at the top.

The <u>names</u> and <u>addresses</u> of your best customers and their past buying information can be worth it's weight in diamonds!

If you know what to do with this list!

Selling is like the ritual of dating — the more you need them — the faster they run.

<u>You must let them come to you</u>. The prospect or customer must "feel" that they need <u>you</u> more than you need them.

→ *Shipped to You for No Cost or Obligation!* Go to: <u>www.PTIW.com/FreeBook</u>

The average business person spends their day *"putting out brush fires"*... Their time and energy gets zapped by all the minor problems that come up from day to day. They are <u>never</u> able to pull back and work on their businesses.

There is no real game plan or strategy!

Many people think they are running their companies — but all they are doing is running the day-to-day operations...

They are locked into survival.

How to write a powerful hard-hitting sales letter:

1. Start with a big promise.
2. Paint the picture.
3. Give them proof.
4. Tell them <u>why</u> it's unique.
5. Close your argument by telling them why they must act now!
6. Make them <u>a</u> very special offer <u>if</u> they respond now!
7. End with a reminder of the promise — summary of offer — and STRONG call for action!

That's it! This is the blueprint or schematic of a sales letter — from start to finish.

❧ Creativity ❧

The creative process is <u>not</u> neat, clean, or pretty. It is not organized. It is dirty, messy, disorganized, and chaotic! It is filled with taking all kinds of unrelated ideas — and <u>mixing them</u> together in a very special way. It is deciding to do something — <u>without</u> knowing how you are going to do it. And then figuring it out as you go!

Roll-Out To Mega Wealth!

The same strategy that generated $1,000.00 can be rolled-out to generate $100,000.00 <u>if</u> the market is big enough — and other factors can be closely matched.

☛ THE HAND ☚

Every offer or promotion must meet these five crucial steps:

1. Is it the right offer?
2. Is it going to the right person?
3. Through the right media?
4. With the right hook?
5. And does it fit together with some kind of long-term plan?

There are only a handful — but they're vital. This lets you focus on the essentials.

<small>(I borrowed this hand concept from *Bill Graham*, the greatest rock-n-roll promoter who ever lived! Bill had his 'handful' of ideas he used for every major event. This let him do BIG THINGS and make quick decisions. It will do the same for you, too!)</small>

Great Quotes:

"People are silently begging to be led."
— *Jay Abraham*

"You can learn more from movement than meditation."
— *Gary Halbert*

"It doesn't have to be good — just good enough."
— *Dan Kennedy*

"All it takes is just one idea to make a million dollars!"
— *Russ von Hoelscher*

"We sell to creatures of emotion — bristling with prejudice — and motivated by pride and vanity."
— *Dale Carnegie*

There is *so much joy* that comes from the long-term effects of a life of <u>hard work</u>, <u>discipline</u>, <u>focus</u>, <u>goal setting</u>, <u>commitment</u>, and <u>daily striving to work towards your dream</u>.

Great Marketers Are Hunters.

We are happiest when we're on the hunt. The bigger the hunt — the happier we are. *We must be reaching all the time.* All is well as long as our reach exceeds our grasp.

→ *Shipped to You for No Cost or Obligation!* Go to: www.PTIW.com/FreeBook

Build "risk reversal" into every offer.

- ★ Risk Reversal is taking all the pressure away from the prospect or customer...
- ★ It's an irresistible guarantee.
- ★ It's a dramatic promise that they must gain a major benefit — or they not only get their money back — but they will also receive something of tremendous value!

This blows them away — and will get you a lot of attention and interest.

Every prospect we seek is running around with a big sign around their neck that is flashing this message:

"Please make me feel important! And good about myself!"

However, only those with trained eyes can see this sign.

Fulfill the strong desire people have to feel...

- Important
- Admired
- Special
- Esteemed
- Beloved
- Observed

And they will give you everything they have!

Direct Mail Marketing is really "Stealth Marketing." *You are flying under the radar!*

None of your competitors ever really know exactly what you're doing! This is a smarter way to do business.

The secret of lead generation: You are now a welcomed guest — <u>not</u> an annoying pest!

- ✓ They sought you out. They are the ones who came to you! You did not go to them!
- ✓ This difference in positioning is everything. It makes them interested, open, and responsive to your sales message.
- ✓ Remember, people like to buy — but they hate being sold. Using lead generation makes them feel in control.

FREE 30-Page Book "Get Paid Every Time Our Phone Rings!" →

Look for things that are <u>HOT</u>!

"Whatever is current creates currency."

<u>STEP ONE</u>:

    Find people to sell shit to.

<u>STEP TWO</u>:

    Find shit to sell to those people!

Marketing is simply a 3-step process:

1. Attracting qualified leads.
2. Converting the highest percentage possible into first-time sales.
3. Re-selling the largest number of customers, as many times as you can, for the highest profit from each sale.

These are the only 3 steps! However, each one must be done the right way.

The best ideas come to you in the heat of the moment!

Write down your best ideas when they are new — and when you are first getting started and very excited!

- <u>These</u> ideas <u>are</u> <u>HOT</u>! You'll need them later on when you are cold!!!
- Ideas are like slippery fish! Hard to hold onto! So you must capture them fast!

❦Cold Calling Sucks!❧

Build a marketing system that automatically brings you qualified prospects that have expressed a great interest and are very likely to buy.

It is <u>not</u> the job of your sales rep to cold-call and develop their own prospects.

→ *Shipped to You for No Cost or Obligation! Go to: www.PTIW.com/FreeBook*

2-Step Marketing is the <u>safest</u> and most profitable way to make money.

STEP ONE: Attract a highly qualified prospect.
- Use a great offer.
- Don't try to sell them too much at first.
- Get your hooks into them.
- Make it as easy as possible for them to buy the first time.
- Sell a low-priced widget.
- Educate them.
- Make them feel that *"They came to you"* — and <u>not</u> the other way around.

STEP TWO: SLAM THEM!
- Now bring out the BIG GUNS!
- You already have their attention and interest... Now you are in the position to show them how you can give them what they desire.

4 stages of learning anything new:

1. **<u>Unconscious</u> <u>Incompetence</u>:** You don't know what you don't know! Total Ignorance!
2. **<u>Conscious</u> <u>Incompetence</u>:** You begin to realize and discover the things you don't know. This is the frustration and confusion period. You're *still* incompetent... But, at least your eyes are beginning to open.
3. **<u>Conscious</u> <u>Competence</u>:** You can function in the new area — but, it's a major struggle — and you're not very good.
4. **<u>Unconscious</u> <u>Competence</u>:** MASTERY! You have mastered the main areas and you do it naturally — like a duck in the water!

Three Proven Ways To Make Money:

1. Do something nobody wants to do.
2. Do stuff others cannot be bothered to do — or would rather not do.
3. Do something you're great at that others are terrible at!!

Business is a combination of:

- ✓ **Art:** We paint the canvas.
- ✓ **War:** Battle the forces!
- ✓ **Science:** Specific tested formulas.
- ✓ **Sport:** Play the game!
- ✓ **Spiritual:** Disciplined. Focused.

The Relationship Model:

1. Think customers — not sales.
2. Build relationships.
3. Spend money consistently to communicate with your customers.
4. Somehow we must convince them that…
   - *We care.*
   - *We want to help.*
   - *We want to serve.*
   - *And do more for them than any competitor.*

Most business owners have no systematic marketing strategy for getting and keeping customers.

They do everything they can think of — and some of what they're doing is working… But most have never thought deeply about the processes — and methods for:

1. Attracting new customers.
2. Selling them for the largest profit.
3. And then re-selling them as often as possible — for the maximum profits.

All of their marketing activities are hit and miss… They never quantify what is working the best. And, without this quantification — they can never combine the best methods into any kind of reliable automatic marketing system.

People are looking for and willing to spend a ton of money for:

The Magic Pill!

This is the product or service that they perceive can instantly and automatically give them something they badly want.

The power of the U.S.P.

(Unique Selling Position)

How can you separate yourself from every other competitor, in the most important way, to your average customer/prospect?

Answer that question in a clear and dramatic way — AND GET RICH!

→ *Shipped to You for No Cost or Obligation! Go to: www.PTIW.com/FreeBook*

Stories **Sell**!

You must create powerful stories that captivate your prospects and customers. These are stories about you, your company, or your products or services.

Choose your stories carefully. They must sound real. They have to be believable and emotional. *There should be some drama!* Some special secret — or a perceived benefit or promise to the reader.

Stories help you make the sale when nothing else will.

Ruthless marketing has nothing to do with ripping people off. In fact, it's just the opposite.

It's all about extracting the largest amount of sales and profits from your targeted marketplace... And to do this — you must re-sell to the largest number of customers.

However, all ruthless marketers are relentless. You must develop the heart of the lion and the mind of the fox! You must be bold and audacious — and a bit cunning in order to seize the greatest opportunities for sales and profits.

It's not about lying to people or cheating them — but it is about mastering the art of getting the largest number of people in your market to give you the largest amount of their disposable income!

Spend one hour a day in concentrated thought of all the ways to build your business.

- ✓ That's 365 focused hours of nothing but thinking and dreaming creatively!
- ✓ One hour a day of doing nothing but focusing on how to build your business will help you dominate your market and destroy your competition!
- ✓ That's over 2 extremely productive weeks a year of nothing but planning — plotting — and scheming!

More Confidence = More Wealth!

From the book *Pour Your Heart Into It*:

"As I proved myself, my confidence grew. Selling, I discovered has a lot to do with self-esteem."

— *Howard Schultz*
CEO of Starbucks

Howard is right!
The harder you work on building yourself — the more money you can make!

A Formula For Creating An Irresistible Offer:

1. Pile high and deeper!
   - *"You'll get this and this and this! And we'll also throw in this, if you act now!"*
   - LOAD IT UP!
   - Offer them a massive amount of stuff for their money!
2. STRONG REASON WHY.
   - There must be a strong reason why you are making them such a powerful offer.
   - The more believable the reason — the more they will respond.
3. Firm Deadline — with a powerful reason why.
   - Everyone has deadlines. The prospect doesn't believe them anymore. You must have a strong reason why the deadline is real.
4. A nice hook.
   - If you're going to create an irresistible offer — it must really be irresistible!
   - The "hook" is the foundation of every offer. It's got to sound really good — or they won't bite.

The key to massive productivity:

Set higher goals!

Commitments, deadlines, responsibilities, and pressures can be your best friend. They force you to do and be more.

Keep the pressure on:

In the midnight hour — when the deadlines are closing in — you are forced to make decisions.

- The walls of indecision begin breaking down.
- And the answers, which were once very muddy, now become clear.

Always begin with the end in mind.

You work backwards...

☆ First, know what you want to accomplish.

☆ Then decide your starting point — and move forward.

You figure it out, shape it, and fine-tune it as you go!

A good direct mail offer is nothing more than a salesman in an envelope.

The really cool thing is:

You can have thousands of these little salesmen working for you every single day!

→ *Shipped to You for No Cost or Obligation!* Go to: www.PTIW.com/FreeBook

Enthusiasm Sells!

If you're excited about what you do — it will attract others... People will gather around to watch you burn!

Enthusiasm makes up for all kinds of defects! After all, everyone loves a truly enthusiastic person.

$ $ $ $ $

To be a super-salesperson you have to believe strongly in whatever you are selling.

Selling is a transference of emotion! You must be sold <u>before</u> you can sell!

A great salesperson cannot make anyone buy something they don't want... That's why we must get prospects to "<u>raise their hand</u>" and show us that they are interested.

- ✓ Let the prospects qualify themselves by jumping through the hoops we hold in front of them!
- ✓ This is the secret to making <u>easy</u> sales!

❦Fail forward!❦

Q. What's the secret of success?

A. Making great decisions.

Q. What's the secret to making great decisions?

A. Make as many bad decisions as you can — as quickly as you can — and learn from them!

Wealth-Builder's Rule #1:

Make damn sure that the bulk of your income is not dependent on the number of actual hours you work. *After all, who makes more money — the brain surgeon or the rock star?*

The "4-M's" to create your own money-machine:

→ **MODELS** — Why create, when you can steal? What works for one will work for you. There are plenty of proven models you can steal from. Do it!

→ **MARKETING** — Attracting prospects and customers! Selling, re-selling, and re-selling again and again!

→ **MARGINS** — Make your promotions fail-proof… even with low response rates! Make your margins high! Higher! Highest!

→ **MANAGEMENT** — Organizing, systematizing, controlling, auto-pilot, absentee ownership mentality.

? ? ? ? ?
Why Direct Mail?

✓ Direct mail can give you tremendous leverage.

✓ Every direct marketing piece is a salesman in an envelope!

✓ It's out there working for you — and making huge numbers of sales, without your direct effort!

✓ Sending out 1,000 direct mail letters is like sending out a sales force of 1,000 of the best salespeople!

The power of take-away selling:

✓ <u>Nothing bothers people more than giving them something they really want</u> — <u>and then threatening to take it away!</u>

✓ The more they want it — and the more they <u>know</u> you can take it away — the more sales and profits you will make!

Great marketers
see opportunities
where others cannot.

→ *Shipped to You for No Cost or Obligation!* **Go to: www.PTIW.com/FreeBook**

If you only knew just how apathetic people are when they read your sales material you'd be shocked!

- ➤ There are exceptions — but most people don't care! They have a great deal of unconscious (or even conscious) resistance against what you are saying.
- ➤ You must be totally aware of this — before you can develop the correct strategies to deal with it.

The power of the 5 A.M. Club:

- ☆ Force yourself to get out of bed before you want to — and put on a big pot of strong black coffee. — Pull out some paper and pens and start writing!
- ☆ Ideas will come to you and through you — that you would never have discovered if you stayed in bed!

There is a magic at work here that's hard to explain! You must experience it — before you can believe it!

Wisdom from a Master Showman:

"It's not the audience who has the power — it's me! It is my talent and ability to know how to keep giving them what they want. I am in control — not them."
— *Johnny Carson*

This is a paradox:

YES, the market comes first. But it's your ability to "read" the market to discover the most powerful and profitable ways to serve it that counts.

The power is in your hands, not theirs.

Creativity comes from the labor of a driven and highly determined person!

Rebelliousness is also a key factor to creativity.

- Think outside the norm of your industry.
- Question everything.
- Be an independent thinker.
- Strive to be different!

Conformity breeds people who are as creative as a head of cabbage!

WE MUST BUY EVERY SALE WE MAKE!!!

✓ We are in the business of buying sales at a profit!

✓ We must constantly spend our money in proven ways that allow us to buy these sales at a profit.

Every new customer must be won! We must do something <u>BOLD</u> to attract them to us.

QUANTITY LEADS TO QUALITY.

The secret to coming up with the greatest ideas is to come up with lots of ideas! Go wild! Don't hold back! Just get into the habit of letting it flow! Set a time every morning for brainstorming as many ideas as you can come up with, make it fun and enjoyable to crank out huge quantities of ideas — *and you'll be amazed at the little gems that come out of this process!*

The art of being wise is the art of knowing what to overlook.

➤ Fight for focus!

➤ Spend the majority of your time on the few projects that can bring you the largest amount of sales and profits.

➤ Ignore the advice from those around you who do not understand the big picture!

➤ <u>Prioritize!</u>

There's a lot of competition for your customers' money. <u>Never forget</u> <u>this</u>. If you can't answer the question: "Why should I give it to *you* and not *your competitor*?" then you don't deserve to be in business.

Just like in sports; the team who wants it more than the other team — wins!

You can <u>never</u> know the true value of something until and unless you compare it with something else.

This is a powerful marketing strategy that you <u>must</u> incorporate into <u>all</u> of your sales material. Find as many ways as possible to associate yourself, your company, and your products and services with other items that have the greatest value in the minds and hearts of the people in your market.

Stay very close to your customer.

Know your customers <u>better</u> than they know themselves. How? By thinking about them all the time and realizing that <u>the real reasons</u> they buy are mostly unconscious.

$ $ $ $ $
You must be a BIG THINKER to make BIG MONEY!

- ✓ First comes the GOAL (the mission, the focus, the target).
- ✓ Then come the specific strategies you will use to achieve this outcome.
- ✓ The why to do something is far more important than the how to do something.
- ✓ Work backwards. Establish the goals and the game plan first — then develop the steps to getting there.

$ $ $ $ $

Business is an amplified lifestyle.

It's life amplified! We deal with <u>more</u> problems, challenges, highs and lows, good times, bad times, headaches and hassles, joys and sorrows <u>in one year</u> than most people live with in an entire lifetime.

FREE 30-Page Book "Get Paid Every Time Our Phone Rings!" →

Business levels the playing field. Anyone with a strong desire to get rich and the willingness to do whatever it takes — CAN GET RICH!

Ideas are slippery fish!

They come in sudden flashes! Write them down — fast!

The greatest entrepreneurs tend to be the worst managers. The skills it takes to build a business are usually the opposite of the skills it takes to manage it.

The best stories to use in your sales material are before-and-after stories.

This is a powerful sales formula. The story tells about the problem and then it introduces the solution. Next it shows the great life-changing benefit. *The reader puts himself into the story and is sold!*

> ✤
>
> **It's always good to have more projects than you can comfortably handle.**
>
> ✤ ✤ ✤

> ◆ ◆ ◆
>
> The real business is between our ears and in our hearts — *not in the office!*
>
> ◆ ◆ ◆

I read a book on survival and it said that the #1 trait of successful survivalists is flexibility. So it is in business. The flexible person bends and adapts. The rest break.

Being flexible is all about: changing, growing, adapting, and moving forward.

Spend more money to make more money:

- ✓ "In direct marketing <u>it's the cost to get the sale</u> — not to make a mailing (or series of mailings) that counts."
  — *Jon Goldman*
- ✓ Many times, the secret is to spend more money, <u>not less</u>. This is especially true when you are making offers to your best prospects and customers.

FREE 30-Page Book "Get Paid Every Time Our Phone Rings!" →

Human beings love to repeat the same behaviors over and over again.

If you can get them to do something one time — you can get them to do it the next time.

⊚⊚⊚⊚⊚
The secret of a good direct mail letter:

It doesn't shout at people — it lures them in.

⊚⊚⊚

Working without a strong model is like... *taking a trip without a map.*

True power **is knowing your strengths and weaknesses.**

Don't lie to yourself about these two areas. Most people tend to overestimate their chances of success and underestimate their chances of failure. You must become stronger in the areas you are already strong in and delegate (not abdicate) your weakest areas.

→ *Shipped to You for No Cost or Obligation!* Go to: www.PTIW.com/FreeBook

Find good people — and stay loyal to them:

It's always easier to maintain a relationship you already have — than to go out and start a new one.

T he insiders are usually blind. Only an outsider can objectively look at something in a fresh, new way.

The <u>easiest thing</u> someone can do is stand on the sidelines and argue for the safe and conservative plan.

It takes a hell of a lot courage to step out and try new things, but this is the only way to build our businesses. *We must be bold!*

Every once in a while you should ask yourself:

"Do I own a business or a job?"

Wisdom from the notorious takeover artist,
T. Boone Pickens:

"Business is not life. Life is tragic. Business is fun! It's like a game you play. It's more like playing a game of racquetball than living life.**"**

We are all self-made... but only the successful will admit it.

When you say, "YES!" to one thing and totally put your heart into it — you are automatically saying "No!" to many other things.

✷ ✷ ✷
The adversities in life can make us stronger... and that's great, because business is a constant adversity.
✷ ✷ ✷

~MOST~ self-employed people **have** a terrible boss!

The only **real power** you have over other people is the power to **influence** or **persuade** them.

You can make more money with 1% of 100 peoples' efforts — *than with 100% of your own individual efforts.*

The 4 laws of self teaching:

1. *You are your greatest teacher.*
2. You can learn <u>anything</u> you want to learn.
3. You <u>must</u> take total responsibility for everything that happens to you.
4. Experience + Reflection = Wisdom!

Step out in faith — and figure it out *as you go!*

The great Olympic runner, Steve Prefontaine said:

"There may be men who can beat me — but they'll have to bleed to do it!"

Product knowledge is highly overrated.

Every salesperson is trained in extensive product knowledge. FORGET THAT! Prospect knowledge is more important than product knowledge. Prospects buy perceived benefits and results. They do not buy product information.

◆ ◆ ◆ ◆ ◆

A successful business is constantly changing, developing, evolving, and growing! It's like a living organism that evolves to meet the demands of the environment.

◆ ◆ ◆ ◆ ◆

→ *Shipped to You for No Cost or Obligation!* Go to: www.PTIW.com/FreeBook

People want to do business with people just like them.

"I have a lot of competition, but ZERO competitors!"

— *Kerry Thomas*

$ $ $

I LIKE DEBT...

Part of the fun is to have the constant pressure to meet your financial obligations.

The carrot and the stick are both great motivators... But the stick is more important!

$ $ $

If your back-end business is strong — you should set out to lose as much money as you possibly can to make the first sale to new customers.

Your first sale sets up all the future sales... The only purpose of your first sale is to build enough relationship with the new customer to get the next sale.

Nothing gives you freedom like having **a few bucks in the bank!**

When asking, <u>ASK</u> <u>**BOLDLY**</u>.

A person's greatest need is to feel appreciated...

You <u>must</u> make them feel important and special and needed — <u>without</u> appearing phony. This is very difficult. But the world's most successful people have mastered this powerful skill.

The power of simplicity:

If you can't sum up your basic offer in one sentence — go back to the drawing board.

→ *Shipped to You for No Cost or Obligation!* **Go to: www.PTIW.com/FreeBook**

All marketing lies in <u>two words</u>:

attraction and retention.

Do everything possible to shift the power and get <u>them</u> to chase <u>you</u> — *rather than you chasing them!*

Are you a professional or an amateur?

The difference: Amateurs only work hard when they feel like it. Professionals work just as hard whether they feel like it or not.

"Marketing is simply a combination of math and psychology."

— *Dan Kennedy*

Our job as marketers is to *attract* the right people and *repel* the wrong ones.

What do all people want? Someone to do it for them! That's why all of us should be in the "do-it-for-em" business!

All this talk about retirement is nonsense! Work gives our lives purpose, meaning, and structure. Stop telling me to take it easy...
I'll have eternity to take it easy!

In business, if you rest, you rust.

→ *Shipped to You for No Cost or Obligation! Go to: www.PTIW.com/FreeBook*

··················
**Does talent create
its own opportunities?**
Or does your total passion and
commitment to the opportunities
create its own talent?
··················

**Neatness rejects
involvement.
Dumb your sales
letters down.**
*Make them
look homely.*

**Key to great
sales material:**

**Write lots of copy
and edit it down.**

**Playing it safe is
no guarantee
against misfortune.**

The way to sell the *unfamiliar* is to link it with the *familiar*.

It's far better to have a friendship that is centered around the business — than to have a business that's centered around a friendship.

Business is at its <u>best</u> when it is honestly selfish. Strive to keep it that way with all your relationships.

Jump — and the net will appear!

- ✓ Make the commitment first.
- ✓ Set the deadline!
- ✓ Run the ad — then scramble to put the fulfillment together!
- ✓ Make <u>BIG</u> <u>PROMISES</u> to groups of customers — and then scramble to make them real!
- ✓ Do whatever you can to force yourself to do more!

The question all marketers <u>must</u> constantly ask:

What's next?

→ *Shipped to You for No Cost or Obligation! Go to: www.PTIW.com/FreeBook*

$ $ $
Happiness is...
a never-ending stream of positive cash-flow!

$ $ $

You must create "Exclusivity."

➤ There <u>must</u> be something that automatically separates you — your company — and the stuff you sell — from all the other competitors.

➤ This "something different" <u>must</u> be very important to your customers — and must be created by you.

Salespeople get paid to hear the word "no!"

A "no" does not mean "no"to the aggressive person who wants the sale!

"When people are free to do as they please, they usually imitate each other."

— *Eric Hoffer*

············⊙⊚⊚⊚⊙············
Retirement = Death.
············⊙⊚⊚⊚⊙············

Constantly look for things that are <u>hot now</u>! Feed the existing hunger in the marketplace! Look for ways to put a new twist on things that are making huge sums of money right now.

"Find a parade and get in front of it."

— *John Carlton*

Residual income is the life-blood of your business.

You <u>must</u> put some consistent thought and action into all the ways and means — to get this type of income flowing through your company.

Better to **strengthen your back** than to lighten your load!

→ *Shipped to You for No Cost or Obligation!* Go to: www.PTIW.com/FreeBook

> **Strive to become the competitor you would hate to compete against!**

Knowing <u>what</u> to do will always make you more money than knowing <u>how</u> to do it.

You can figure out all the details later — or better yet — *let someone else figure them out.*

The secret to making <u>more money</u> in your business can be summed up in two words:

☞ THINK BIGGER! ☜

- ✓ You gotta keep your eye on the multi-million dollar (or billion!) prize!
- ✓ You <u>must</u> be willing to walk over a lot of $100.00 bills to get to the millions or billions you want.
- ✓ In other words, it's a fight for FOCUS! You must constantly put all of your time, attention, energy, and resources on the areas that can make you the most money.

The heart rules the mind! (That's why we <u>must</u> sell to their emotions!)

FREE 30-Page Book "Get Paid Every Time Our Phone Rings!" →

In any negotiation...

The person who pretends like they need or want it <u>the</u> <u>least</u> — **WINS!**

Let your communications buzz with excitement!

The <u>greatest sin of all</u> is to bore somebody!

The value of an employee is determined by 2 things:

1. How much money they <u>directly</u> bring into the company? (In other words, without their <u>direct</u> effort — this money would not have come in.)
2. How difficult will they be to replace?

Nothing else matters.

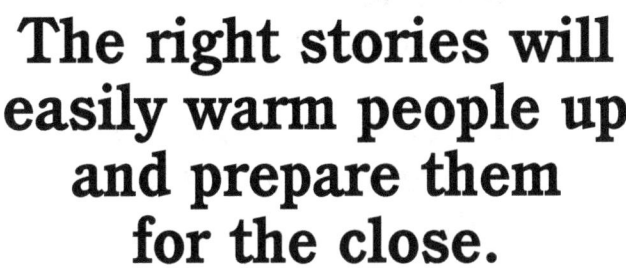

The right stories will easily warm people up and prepare them for the close.

❧❧❧

"You must enter the conversation that's already in their mind."

— *Robert Collier*

Every great story has two essential elements: TENSION & DISCOVERY.

It's all about pressure and release! Build the pressure, create the tension, make it real, and <u>then introduce the discovery</u>! *Now you can sell them!*

An entrepreneurial rule for choosing new ventures:

In any new business venture — if it's not a stretch — don't do it! It must scare you and induce some risk. <u>If not, don't do it.</u>

❦❦❦❦❦

Take good care of the people who take good care of you!

❦❦❦

❦❦❦

Put your entire focus on making a BIGGER PIE — not on counting and weighing each slice!

All growth comes from consciously living outside of your comfort zone.

If you're not doing things on a regular basis that scare you just a little (or a lot!) — you're not growing.

Everybody loves an offer they perceive is just for them.

The things they want the most are the things others cannot get!

━━━━━❧❦☙━━━━━

Success is the ability to outrun failure!

"Business is a good game — lots of competition and a minimum of rules. You keep score with the money."
— *Nolan Bushnell*

The Power of Focus…

Don't spend your time managing problems. Spend your time building your opportunities.

The best marketing is <u>always</u> in a constant state of flux.

Most people are secretly looking for someone to lead them by the hand.

> **You serve yourself best — *when you serve others the most.***

Your marketing (everything you do to get more customers and keep them spending more money for life) is only limited by your imagination.

Remember that every time you are going through a sales slump or a cash-flow crisis.

Keep feeding the fire of your enthusiasm — so it <u>always</u> burns brightly!

- ✓ Get involved in exciting new projects that stir your blood!
- ✓ Stay excited about the future!
- ✓ Set bigger goals and grander visions!
- ✓ "If you want to turn your hours into minutes, renew your enthusiasm!" — *Papyrus*

You can't have the glory... IF YOU DON'T HAVE THE GUTS!

→ *Shipped to You for No Cost or Obligation!* **Go to: www.PTIW.com/FreeBook**

People hate to be "sold" — but they love to "choose."

Spend more money — to close more sales!

1. You can't go wrong if you are spending this money on super qualified prospects.
2. You are selling big ticket items with good margins.

In some cases (as long as your percentage of conversion is going up) you can't spend too much money!

Keep searching for products and services with the largest gap between perceived value and actual cost.

➤ These are the items that can make you rich!

➤ Look for items where the prospect doesn't know or care about your actual cost.

Customers go where they are invited and stay where they are appreciated.

> **After a while, you STOP listening to what other people say — and *only* pay attention to what they do.**

Think of the groups of leads you attract into your business as a HUGE TON of dirt, mud, and rocks — <u>with</u> <u>a</u> <u>few</u> <u>solid</u> <u>gold</u> <u>nuggets</u> mixed in with all this filth! Your job is to keep sifting through all the mud and crap to find these gold nuggets!

You must sift through this rubble in the cheapest possible way — so the <u>majority</u> of your marketing costs can be invested in the gold nugget group — not the muddy group!

Most marketers are weak.

- ◆ They quit way too soon.
- ◆ They are too worried about offending their prospects or customers.
- ◆ Or, they simply don't know that there is a great deal more money laying on the table that could and should be theirs — if they simply went after it more aggressively and then stayed after it until they got it!

"The most important thing in life is not to capitalize on your gains. Any fool can do that! The really important thing is to profit from your losses. That requires intelligence and it makes the difference between a wise man and a fool."

William Boltho, Twelve Against the Gods

→ *Shipped to You for No Cost or Obligation! Go to: www.PTIW.com/FreeBook*

❋ ❋ ❋

Take away selling:

Sometimes when you say "No!" — it only makes them want you more!

❋ ❋ ❋

Continuing to make <u>BIG MONEY</u> over a period of years never happens by accident. It is *always* the result of high intention, sincere effort, intelligent direction, and skillful execution. It represents the wise choices of many alternatives and the cumulative experience you gain from all the years of disciplined and focused work.

"I've seen companies so obsessed with competition that they keep looking in their rearview mirror and crash into a tree."

— *Sergey Brin*
Co-Founder of Google.com

Create as many "businesses within your business" as you possibly can.

Go out of your way to show people that you are <u>REAL</u> and vulnerable — and they will emotionally open up to you.

Love and hate play an important role in the creative process.

- To begin a project — you must fall completely and totally in love with it! And while in love — write <u>all</u> of the promotional materials!
- And to complete the project — you must <u>hate</u> <u>it</u> in the worst way and want nothing more than to be done with it so you can move on to something else!

A good direct-response follow-up sequence works like the Chinese torture method where you are strapped to a table and a small drop of water hits your forehead every two seconds. After a while you go mad!

A good follow-up campaign does the same thing: <u>It breaks down the sales resistance of your prospects</u>. After a while they say, "NO MORE! You've got me! Count me in — here's my money!"

Get your *best offer* in front of <u>more people</u> and follow-up like crazy!

→ *Shipped to You for No Cost or Obligation!* **Go to: www.PTIW.com/FreeBook**

The best product does not always win, *but the best marketing always does!*

Most people run their businesses like a person who drives with one foot on the gas pedal and the other foot on the brake pedal!

What a joke! A better analogy to run your business is the way champion race car drivers win their races: all of their attention and energy is focused on the road ahead. They only think of winning and their concentration is totally in the moment.

Damn the critics!

- The critics of this world are little-thinkers who are controlled by their doubts and fears.
- They love to pick a new idea apart — but often all they do is analyze it to death!
- These people think they are being smart — but what they are really doing is thinking small. Their entire focus is on the difficulties rather than the possibilities.
- The bottom line: It's easier to criticize. It's easier to think small and look for all the things that can go wrong. This type of thinking requires zero courage.
- Great companies die because the BIG thinking action-oriented entrepreneurs who built them are replaced by "middle managers" who love to sit around and have meetings and discuss what they're going to talk about at the next meeting.
- They see all the risks and do nothing.

Negative motivation often works much better than anything positive!

The stick is always better than the carrot!

▪ ▪ ▪
The mass of men are usually wrong about everything!

Do the opposite of what everyone else does and you will almost always succeed!

▪ ▪

Every business deal is always much easier to get into than to get out of...

- ❖ Especially for those of us who are eternal optimists!
- ❖ So please try to think everything through as clearly as possible from all angles — while you are high on the idea.
- ❖ How does it fit with your BIGGER plan?
- ❖ What are the exit strategies?
- ❖ What happens if it doesn't work out?
- ❖ The answers to these questions can save you years of heartache.

Whoever said: "Do what you love and the money will follow" was wrong! It should be:

"<u>Learn</u> to love the activities that are capable of producing the largest sum of money — and the money will follow!"

Your business is like a bicycle. Either you keep it moving or you fall down!

- ★ Keep searching for your next big winner!
- ★ Keep finding better ways to give your customers and prospects what you know they want the most!

→ *Shipped to You for No Cost or Obligation!* Go to: www.PTIW.com/FreeBook

Use more premiums to drive your sales and profits!
Here's how:

1. Choose or develop the ultimate premium of the greatest value to your market.
2. Sell the FREE premium! Make it the star of your show!
3. The only catch: The product or service comes along with your FREE premium on a trial basis.
4. Let them keep the premium if they return the item you are selling.

Great premiums work because:

a. They overcome the apathetic laziness and fear that most prospects feel when they see your pitch.
b. If you choose the right premium — they let you harness the power of greed!

Objections are great!

- ◈ Never run from objections. You can turn each one into a solid reason for buying!
- ◈ List every single possible objection. Then create a multi-page report called: "Your BIGGEST Questions Answered!" Each question is an objection. Your answer erases every possible doubt in their minds.

Life, love, and business favor the bold!

Revolution accelerates evolution!

→ Be bold and innovative!
→ Test your wildest ideas!
→ Experiment like crazy!
→ Radical change is the key to discovering new ideas that can make you rich! Keep your business in a state of constant flux. *Make "change" your #1 product.*

$ $ $ $ $
What you sell and what you "really" sell are two different things.

- "In our factory, we make lipstick. In our advertising, we sell hope." — *Charles Revlon*
- "Kodak sells film, but they don't advertise film. They advertise memories." — *Theodore Levitt*
- What you "really" sell is all that touch-feely emotional crap that you must connect to whatever gizmo you're pushing.

$ $ $ $ $

◈◈◈◈◈
Wise men have <u>many</u> doubts.
◈◈◈◈◈

Stay very focused on your market every day and you will be in the market for many years! Your market is your meal ticket for life!

The #1 reason that the most solid businesses begin to decline is simply because they <u>STOP</u> doing the things that took them to the top.

- ◆ They lose their edge.
- ◆ They lose their focus.
- ◆ They lose their hunger.
- ◆ They lose the boldness and creativity they had when they were struggling their way to the top. They become conservative and complacent. Now they are easy targets for all of the others who are just like they once were!

Don't try to figure things out too quickly. Let your ideas have time to ferment.

- The best ideas for building your business are like all of the ingredients you put in the pot when you're making chili. Any good cook will tell you that the "secret" is not only adding the right ingredients — but letting it stew.
- Great ideas are like this, too.
- You must be willing to go through the pain of confusion. You <u>must</u> suffer through many twists and turns along the path — to get to your final destination. It's 3 steps forward and 2 steps back all along the way. You are constantly stumbling around in the dark looking for the light switch!

Because so many people these days are skeptical — and so many marketers are lying every time they open their mouths — <u>you can use brutal honesty</u> as your marketing weapon!

Tell them what to do — *but not how to do it!*

General George Patton had one simple rule for warfare that works like magic in business. **Every battle plan must be carried out with 3 things:**

- ➤ <u>Speed!</u>
- ➤ <u>Simplicity!</u>
- ➤ <u>Boldness!</u>

Your marketing plans must incorporate these 3 elements. Strike FAST, strike HARD, and strike OFTEN!

FREE 30-Page Book "Get Paid Every Time Our Phone Rings!" ➔

Money may not make you happy… but it will help calm your nerves!

It's always better to have it and not need it than to need it and not have it!

"The gold is in your existing clients."

—*Joe Polish*

Business is a lot like that popular reality show on TV — "Survivor." The object of that game is to:

- Outwit
- Outlast, and
- Outplay your competition!

We <u>must</u> do this, too!

No matter what you sell — there's always some part of it that you can give away for free.

→ By doing this — you make people feel like they owe <u>you</u> something in return. Now they are ready and willing to listen to what you have to say. And if you do it right — you will make them see the value of whatever you're selling and make them want to pay you the full price for it.

→ Offering them something for free wakes them up! It makes it super easy for serious prospects to raise their hand and say, "Okay, give it to me now!" It separates <u>you</u> from all the other competitors who *never* do this. And it gets you in the door and makes it so simple and easy to sell them!

→ *Shipped to You for No Cost or Obligation! Go to: www.PTIW.com/FreeBook*

People are much more *influenced* by the height of your enthusiasm than the depth of your knowledge.

All business is *show business!*

◆ ◆ ◆ ◆ ◆

Love will find a way — indifference will find an excuse.

- ✓ Learn to love the things you do that bring you the largest number of sales and profits!
- ✓ Love makes all burdens light. This is the key to doing your <u>best</u> work!

◆ ◆ ◆ ◆ ◆

Your best customers are like fires. They go out if unattended.

→ The key word is "relationship."

→ The better they "feel" about you — the more money they will give you!

→ Remember, the fire never dies as long as you keep feeding it!

"What are you willing to do?"

The answer to these six words will determine how much money you will ultimately make.

Catch yourself on fire and they will come to watch you burn!

Winston Churchill said it best:

"Before you can inspire with emotion, you must be swamped with it yourself."

Many business people who pride themselves greatly for being very conservative in the way they carefully think everything through — are not conservative at all. <u>They're</u> <u>scared</u>!

- They think they're being careful, but what they are really doing is being totally controlled by fear and limited thinking.

- For every wild-eyed big-thinking entrepreneur who blows up their company because of their reckless actions — there are probably 100,000 business people who are playing it *way too safe* and losing out on all kinds of money that could and should be theirs.

The marketers' <u>most</u> <u>important</u> <u>asset</u> is his or her knack for putting themselves in the position of their customers and for addressing *their* most important needs.

→ *Shipped to You for No Cost or Obligation!* **Go to: www.PTIW.com/FreeBook**

There is no beginning, middle, and end to the creative process.

- ◆ Your best ideas will evolve as you move forward!
- ◆ Each new idea can be the seed for many new ideas.
- ◆ Your <u>best</u> <u>work</u> is *always* still out there!

Your personal stories are <u>the</u> <u>best</u> <u>way</u> to drive home your strongest selling messages.

- ◈ Your stories contain emotional power!
- ◈ They bypass the prospect's brain and go right to the heart!
- ◈ Your best prospects will not only remember your main stories, they will be able to repeat them back to you in exact detail!
- ◈ Your best stories will become a strong bond that <u>will</u> connect you to your prospect!
- ◈ Your stories are 100% proprietary! They are yours and yours alone. *Only you are uniquely qualified to tell your stories.* This is your best way to separate yourself from your other competitors and gain a foothold into the minds and hearts of the people in your market.

"The road to excess leads to enlightenment!"
— *William Blake*
(A man who pushed the envelope!)

- ✓ You <u>never</u> know how far you can go until and unless you push yourself way too far!
- ✓ You push it hard — until it breaks — then fix it — then push it even harder, until it breaks again!
- ✓ Whoever said, "Don't bite off more than you can chew," was wrong! The secret to wealth is to constantly be involved in way more projects than you can possibly handle! You must boldly push beyond your limits in order to expand them. The higher you climb, the more you can see… SO KEEP CLIMBING HIGHER!

NEVER promote a product or service that you can't explain in 3 minutes!

- ▣ Or at least cover the major benefits!
- ▣ Does this sound impossible? It's not! Genius is the art of making complicated things "seem" simple.

"As I proved myself, my confidence grew. Selling, I discovered has a lot to do with self-esteem."

— *Howard Schultz,
CEO of Starbucks*

Howard is right! The harder you work on building yourself — the more money you can make!

Make your sales material *outrageous!*

- Do not be afraid to make it bigger and bolder!
- Make it louder!
- Make it somewhat controversial.
- Too much of the sales material I see is neat, clean, pretty, carefully written, and boring as hell! You must dare to be different! WAKE THEM UP! Don't be afraid of offending people. In fact, you must offend the wrong people to attract the right ones!

Customers are and will always be totally self-centered.
They don't care about you.
Never have. Never will.
They only care about what you can do for them — better, faster, and less expensively.

We all write "Dear Friend" when addressing our customers — but in reality, they are not our friends.
They are demanding tyrants who must be served!

The **true art** of selling is to make people feel that they are the ones chasing you!

To be very aggressive with your marketing <u>without</u> appearing like you need or even care whether they do business with you.

→ *Shipped to You for No Cost or Obligation!* Go to: www.PTIW.com/FreeBook

Find the buyers who can buy the most and you won't have to find the most buyers!

Less is more!

If you only knew just how apathetic people are when they read your sales material you'd be shocked!

- There are exceptions — but most people don't care! They have a great deal of unconscious (or even conscious) resistance <u>against</u> what you are saying.

- You must be totally aware of this — <u>before</u> you can develop the correct strategies to deal with it.

Who are your real enemies? They're <u>not</u> who you think!

→ Your real enemies are the people who tell you what you want to hear and completely agree with everything you do. They try to pump your ego — pat you on the back — laugh at your stupid jokes — and all the other "yes-men."

→ These people are your enemies because they will lull you to sleep if you let them. They will pull you down into the quicksand of smugness and self-satisfaction. Because of this — you will lose your edge.

→ What you need are people who will get in your face and tell you that you are wrong! People who challenge you and stimulate you into taking new actions and striving to do and become more than you are now!

In good times and bad, there will *always* be a market for things that nobody needs!

If you want to eek out a comfortable living, sell things that people need.

If you want to get rich — sell things that people want!

MONEY IS LIKE MANURE...

You gotta spread it around and mix it up in some good soil and throw in the right seeds — otherwise it is worthless.

- If you pile it up and don't use it — it stinks!
- Keep spreading it around in as many things as possible that keep you excited and moving forward.

Joe Karbo's famous headline reads: "Most people are too busy making a living to get rich." He couldn't have been more right!

➤ The majority are prisoners of petty thinking. They go through life asking for so little. Their priorities are all screwed up!

➤ There are so many forces against the ambitious person who wants to make many millions of dollars.

Blow your own horn!

Nobody's going to blow your horn for you — you gotta get out there and do it!

The "perception" that you always have something "new" and exciting to share with them is one of the things that will *always* keep them coming back for more!

✴ What messages can you send out to your market that keeps them eager to hear from you?

✴ How can you keep it "fresh" in the minds and hearts of your older and more established core customers who have already heard your story a million times?

Carlos Gambino, the powerful Mob boss, rose from the bottom to the top with this simple philosophy:

"Have the heart of the lion and the mind of the fox."

Qualities of THE LION:

Powerful • Forceful • Strong • King of the Jungle • Killer (but also playful) • Brave • Independent • Agile • Fearless

Qualities of THE FOX:

Careful • Cunning • Smart • Invisible • Elusive • Fast • Shrewd

The lion is the king of the jungle and roars loudly! The fox is hard to spot and catch! He is quick and smart.

This simple philosophy not only made Carlos Gambino the most powerful Mob boss ever — but he never spent a day of his life in jail!

Blur the lines between <u>work</u> and <u>play</u>.

Database marketing in 3 words:

★ **Segment**

★ **Concentrate**

★ **Dominate!**

Wisdom from rock-n-roll hall of famer, Tom Petty (one of the most successful and prolific singer/songwriters in history):

"Other people take vacations and go to Hawaii and play golf or scuba dive. This is what I do. I write songs and I make records."

→ Stay 100% focused on your work. Master it. Let it become the best part of who you are. Stay totally committed to becoming the <u>best</u> you can be. Fall in love with what you do! And always strive to become even better.

→ This is the closest thing to true happiness I have ever discovered.

Here is one of my favorite quotes that is right next to my big clock, so I can see it all the time:

❝ Business is <u>always</u> a struggle. There are always obstacles and competitors. There is never an open road, except the wide road that leads to failure. Every great success has always been achieved by fight. Every winner has scars. Those who succeed are the efficient few. They are the few who have the ambition and willpower to develop themselves. **❞**

— *Herbert N. Casson*

Your goal for each day is to come up with <u>at least</u> <u>one</u> <u>new</u> <u>idea</u> that you *didn't* have yesterday for increasing your sales and profits!

The <u>golden key</u> to burnout is to fall back in love with your work.

ಌಌ

What were the things that pumped you up in the beginning? Why did you love them? How can you fill your life with more of the things that excited you the most?

The true secret of success is to be bold and tenacious!

Put it all out there. <u>Don't</u> hold back even for a single second. Express yourself fully — to the point of being totally outrageous! Mix this with a high degree of tenacity and you'll shoot straight to the top! Nothing can hold you back as long as you have these two qualities. You will leapfrog over all those cold and timid souls who <u>never</u> put their whole heart and soul into <u>anything</u> and then give up at the first sign of adversity.

"Give a man enough audacity and tenacity and he will surely rule the world."

— *Marcus Aurelius*

→ *Shipped to You for No Cost or Obligation! Go to: www.PTIW.com/FreeBook*

◈ ◈ ◈ ◈ ◈

Never fear objections! *Bring 'em on!*

◈ ◈ ◈

"Most people would kill just to be treated like a god for only one brief moment."

— *Gene Hackman's character from the movie "Hoosiers"*

The only 3 ways to make money:

1. <u>Sell your time for money</u>. You charge by the hour and trade your life for a paycheck.
2. <u>Sell a product or service</u>. Your money comes from the sale of the gizmo — not the time or work it takes to sell it.
3. <u>Passive income</u>. Your money makes you more money <u>without</u> your direct effort. All of the world's richest people make their money with the third method. Their money comes to them automatically from a wide variety of cash-producing investments. Their money keeps making them more money! Do everything you can to make as much of your money as possible in the third area! What would you rather be: A rock star or a brain surgeon?

◈ ◈ ◈ ◈ ◈

The best sales material is like fine wine — it needs time to age.

◈ My best sales promotions have one thing in common — they are jobs that took two or three weeks to do. I let my best ideas grow and take on a life of their own.

◈ I worked on them slowly and figured it all out as I went along. It took some time to do all of this — but the results speak for themselves. Of course, now you can always go back and re-write this letter over and over again! So what took you weeks can <u>now</u> be re-done in a matter of days or even hours!

"When you advertise fire extinguishers, open with the fire."

Advertising Legend,
— David Ogilvy

No matter how bad your business may be right now — as long as you have a huge list of customers — you are <u>always</u> only one irresistible offer away from making bazillions of dollars!

Most people are penny wise and dollar foolish.

◆ They're walking over the dollars to get to the dimes!

◆ It's so insane, and yet I see this crazy behavior manifested in a multitude of ways.

◆ These people lack vision. They just can't see the BIG PICTURE. They are totally controlled by their fear, greed, and stupidity.

The easy way to dramatically increase your persuasive power: <u>WRITE</u> <u>MORE</u>!

➤ Consistent writing about your #1 subject helps to crystalize your thinking.

➤ This, in turn, <u>will</u> make you a much more persuasive thinker. You will speak with greater confidence and power. Your ideas will be sharper and more people will want to buy and re-buy from you.

➜ *Shipped to You for No Cost or Obligation! Go to: www.PTIW.com/FreeBook*

Problems and pain ARE GOOD THINGS!

Competitive people see problems and pain as challenges. *They use the pressure of adversity to spur them on to new heights!*

What drives you?

Knowing the right answer to this question can make you more money, faster and easier than you think! Here are the six main needs that "drive" all of us. The need for:

1. Variety
2. Stability
3. Love/Connection
4. Significance
5. Growth
6. Contribution

Discover the true secrets behind your most powerful motivations in life... And then look for <u>all</u> the ways you can fill your life with as many of these things as possible.

Your Hour of Profit Power!

The best thing you can do to dramatically increase your sales and profits is to spend at least ONE SOLID HOUR each day — first thing in the morning — where you think about nothing except all the various ways you can sell more stuff to your marketplace.

Prosperity consciousness and "new age thinking" sounds great — but most new age thinkers I know are always broke!

Why is this?

Happiness lies in the relentless pursuit of profits!

- ✓ The thrill is in the hunt, not the catch!
- ✓ Keep searching for newer and better ways to make more money!
- ✓ Turn all of your money-getting activities into a game that you play — for the sake of playing!
- ✓ Making money really is the greatest game on earth!

Street-smart business rule: Take good care of the people who are taking good care of you!

- ➤ Surround yourself with the best people you can find. Then don't run them off!
- ➤ The best employee is often a combination of several of them.

You can't teach people how to be wise. This is something that <u>must be earned</u> over a period of time.

- Facing all the problems — moving forward year after year — in spite of all the obstacles.
- Living through some terribly painful times.
- Discovering what you *hate* and *don't want*. (Much more important than what you do want.)
- Not giving up when any other sane and rational person would.

Manipulation can be a damn good thing.

The <u>best</u> things in my life started out being nothing more than delusions... I thank God for all the people who have lied to me about how simple and easy it would be to get rich, become a master copywriter, write books, have a happy marriage, and all the other things I have paid such a huge price for. Had I known how difficult these things were to achieve, I would have never started!

The more money a customer spends — the less problems they cause you.

There are exceptions to this, but they are few and far between. The BIGGEST pain in the ass customers are almost always the ones who spend the least amount of money.

Not making enough money?

★ Your sales and profits are not high enough?

★ IT'S YOUR OWN FAULT!

★ The day you accept full responsibility for all the money you do or don't make is also the day you can begin to turn everything around.

"Consumption expands with usage."
— *Dan Kennedy*

I used to worry that I was trying to sell too much stuff to my customers. Now I only worry that I'm not selling them enough stuff!

Dependable monthly income sets you free!

→ Especially if you don't have to do much (or even anything!) to keep it coming in!

→ Strive to create as many of these types of opportunities as possible!

Massive action solves ALL personal financial problems!

- Turn up the volume!
- Start moving in 40 directions at once!
- Find the things that produce the biggest results and then repeat them in the biggest way you can!

"The closer you get to the ultimate goal, the less exciting it is."
— *Neil Young*

Robert J. Ringer's 3 simple money making rules:

1. If you want more, make yourself worth more.
2. Concentrate on quality and service <u>first</u>, and profit will automatically follow.
3. Always give people more than you expect to get in return.
   - Out of these 3, I believe #1 is more important than the other 2 combined!
   - The more you do to make yourself worth more (even if it is only hype and bullshit — such as writing a bunch of books!), the more money you <u>will</u> automatically make.

Unreasonable people rule the world!

All great entrepreneurs are a bit unreasonable!

Great entrepreneurs love change.
We embrace it! We need it.
We crave it. The rest of the world is our <u>exact</u> opposite in this regard.

What something costs is not the issue. The only thing that matters is the profit you make.

- Many times you must spend more money to make more money.
- It takes more money, not less, to do the things that are necessary to completely separate yourself from all of your competitors and shock all of your best prospects and customers.
- A fatal sin we all commit (even those of us who know better) is to hold back when we should be giving and doing more.
- Spending more money to convert sales does not have to be risky. You can test small — and let the numbers prove that this is the better move that "will" make you more money. Only then will you commit to spending the BIG BUCKS. However, even then, you can closely monitor each campaign and STOP spending all this extra money whenever you see your profits declining.

❝There are only two things that will make you money in any business: marketing and innovation. Everything else is a business expense.❞

— *Management Guru, Peter Drucker*

This quote should be on every business owner's desk — on their bathroom mirror and hanging from their rear view mirror while they drive. Let's all beat it into our heads! Then make sure we spend the maximum amount of time, work, and money in both of these areas today!

To some degree, it's all a numbers game. Be very persistent and don't give up!

Remember the old sales adage, "Some will, some won't. So what? Who's next?"

Timid salespeople raise skinny kids.

Victor Hugo (the great French revolutionist) once said, *"Those who live are those who fight!"*

He's right! The day you stop fighting is the day you begin to die. This is true for your life and for the life of your business.

If you don't know it can't be done, you can do it.

An educated person will stay up all night and worry about things that most of us never even think about. We are too damn busy doing the deal to worry about anything.

Should you write naked?

I once heard a respected marketer say that he only writes copy when the moon is full. He claimed this gave him the power he needed to put the right words on paper. At first I thought he was joking. When I realized he wasn't I said out loud, "That's the stupidest thing I have ever heard!" Now I'm not so sure... You see, writing is a <u>deeply personal activity</u> and there is no one way to do it. The real secret is to experiment with many different things, find out what works best for you, and then do them on a regular basis.

Most ads and sales letters are boring as hell!

They deliver zero "sales performance." They are painful to read… there's no excitement factor… zero enthusiasm… and nothing that compels the prospect to go through the <u>time</u> and <u>trouble</u> to read it.

The <u>why</u> to do something always comes before the <u>how</u> to do it!
This is the secret behind all great achievers.

Great achievers set the goal — and then figure it out as they go along. You can't let a little thing like not knowing how you're going to do something stop you!

❖❖❖

Diversity in your marketing leads to stability in your business. Hit 'em hard. Hit 'em often. <u>Hit 'em many different ways!</u>

❖❖❖

❝The writer who gets things done is the writer who shows up for work day in and day out… Regular hours and regular production are the keys to productivity. The hare may show a lot of early form, but the smart money's always on the tortoise.❞

— *Lawrence Block from the book, "Telling Lies For Fun And Profit"*

Never Fear Objections.

Don't hide! Be upfront about the skepticism you know they feel... Bring up the biggest objections yourself. Then overcome them one by one. You'll win their trust and respect — and you'll get their money.

The best prospects have major objections that must be faced head-on and not skated around.

THE SECRET OF SELF-PROMOTION:

YOU ARE WHO YOU SAY YOU ARE!

Niche Marketing:

Spending <u>more</u> money to reach fewer people. Fewer people that are highly qualified and more likely to buy.

The path of least resistance leads to a life of mediocrity. But, when given two choices — people will always take that path. They'll always take the easiest way... It's human nature.

Test small, *but aggressively.*

You can lose money on 9 out of 10 tests and <u>still</u> make millions by rolling out the 1 winner!

◆ ◆ ◆

You'll never find your greatest winners without aggressive testing.

Every new customer is an investment toward future profits!

Nothing great was never accomplished by business owners whose goal was "<u>slow controlled growth</u>."

We have the power to influence the people we sell to!

Our success is not dependent on the market we serve — nearly as much as it is in our ability to know how to continually give this market what they want.

Get the word 'problem' out of your vocabulary...

There's no such thing as problems — *there are only opportunities and challenges!*

The pain of discipline <u>hurts less</u> than the pain of regret.

Make your high price seem cheap — by comparing it against something much more expensive!

Forbes Ley says that the #1 reason people buy almost anything and everything is because somehow they believe it will help them feel better about themselves.

— $ $ $ —

Relationship Marketing:

Win their hearts — then win their pocketbooks!

— $ $ $ —

Motivation is an internal thing. <u>Nobody can give it to you</u>.

You must keep looking for reasons to win!

"Man inhabits a world of delusion."

— *Edward De Ropp*

People buy cures — not prevention.

They'll spend their life-savings on a wild cure, but little or nothing on prevention.

The wise marketer sees the connections between many different things.

Test everything!

Sometimes it takes a lot of wrong answers to get to the right ones.

Isn't it stupid to spend your valuable time doing the things that others can do <u>faster</u> — <u>easier</u> — and <u>better</u> than you?

People who are great at making excuses — **are often lousy at making money.**

→ *Shipped to You for No Cost or Obligation!* **Go to: www.PTIW.com/FreeBook**

Game Theory for Marketers:

"Game Theory" is the latest buzz of the academic community. Highly educated people have made quite a study of this new area. The concept is simple: "Put yourself into a position that you <u>don't</u> want to be in and then rescue yourself!" In the process of doing this, you discover <u>many</u> interesting things. When I first read about this I said to myself, "This is what all great entrepreneurs have been doing since the beginning of time!" *It's true!* We constantly force ourselves to tap into parts of ourselves that we don't normally reach by constantly biting off way more than we can chew! We back ourselves into corners and then <u>fight</u> <u>our</u> <u>way</u> <u>out</u>!

✯✯✯✯✯✯✯✯✯

One ounce of cure will <u>always</u> outsell 1,000 pounds of prevention!

✯✯✯✯✯✯✯✯✯

If you don't take large risks, you'll <u>never</u> make great gains.

Of course, there are plenty of ways you can test small — *but VERY AGGRESSIVELY!*

◆ STOP LOWERING ◆ YOUR PRICES!

Low prices are reserved for people who <u>cannot</u> market themselves effectively. If you're competing on price, you haven't established enough value in the minds of your prospective customers. It's up to you to prove — without a doubt — that the best prospective buyers in your market should be giving more of their money to you. Marketing is all about differentiation, but it's up to you to create those perceptions of difference in the minds of the people you most want on your customer list.

People re-buy the most by selling them the same way you sold them before.

Spend <u>more</u> money to attract the <u>smaller</u> group of the prime prospects you most want as long-term customers.

When you find your successful formula — don't change it!

...At least until the numbers start going downhill.

Until then, keep finding as many ways as you can to continue making as much money as possible with the same formula that has worked so well for you.

The role of the "visionary" in <u>every progressive company</u> is to believe it BIGGER and see it SIMPLER than ever before!

A direct mail secret.

Direct mail will bring you significantly better customers than <u>any</u> <u>other</u> <u>media</u>. This is especially true when compared to mediums such as the Internet. With direct mail you get what you pay for. Sure, it's expensive, but the end result is the fact that you end up with customers who end up being worth a whole lot more money.

Isn't this what it's all about?

If copy is king — then readability is the queen!

If you <u>can't</u> get them to read it — nobody will buy. You <u>must</u> do everything possible to BREAK UP YOUR WRITING.

A. It must be perceived as easy to read. No BIG BLOCKS or pages of tiny fonts.

B. It must be <u>jagged</u> and <u>never smooth</u>.

C. Each page of your sales letter must somehow "look and feel" different from the preceding page.

D. You <u>must</u> do anything and everything to make it look inviting and interesting.

Involvement is the key... You must do as many things as possible to get and then keep them involved. The deeper they go — the more power you will have to convince them to give you their money.

If your customers want to buy rocks... <u>then start digging!</u>

Most marketers are trying too hard to sell people the things that <u>they</u> want to sell... **instead of just selling what their market wants to buy.**

Seasoned marketers are the <u>most</u> guilty of this. They believe their marketing skills are powerful enough to sell anything to anyone!

"Certainty is hugely seductive."

— *Anthony Starr*

One thing people really want is certainty in an uncertain world. They want to be near someone who they feel has <u>all</u> <u>the</u> <u>answers</u>... Someone who has it all figured out and will now take care of them.

SPEED

Being *faster* is more important than being perfect!

A half-baked idea well executed is much better than that "perfect" idea that is always just around the corner!

Why work when you're already worth $100 million dollars?

"You have got to be, wild guess, worth somewhere north of 100 million dollars. Why are you still touring? You don't have to do this," Scott Pelley remarked in a *60 Minutes* interview with Bruce Springsteen (originally aired October 7, 2007).

"What else would I do? You got any clues?" Springsteen asks. "Got any suggestions? I mean, am I going to garden? Why would you stop. I mean, you play the music and, you know, grown men cry. And women dance. That's why you do it."

The bottom line: You gotta do what makes you feel most alive or most fulfilled... and then find a way to get paid a lot of money for doing it!

Do the things that scare you and you will have the power!

- ◆ Once you go through the terror a bunch of times, you are not nearly as afraid!
- ◆ In fact, many times your fear turns into excitement!
- ◆ You simply re-direct your fearful energy and use it for all kinds of good things.
- ◆ And there is no greater feeling than the one you get when you MASTER YOUR BIGGEST FEARS!

Keep hunting for your next big idea. You never know when or where you'll find it.

Viagra was a heart medication — still in its testing phase — when some researcher took note of a very interesting side effect!

→ *Shipped to You for No Cost or Obligation! Go to: www.PTIW.com/FreeBook*

A secret from one of the wealthiest men in history:

"There is no secret about success. Success simply calls for hard work, devotion to your business at all times, day and night."

— *Henry Clay Frick*

Be thankful for all of your burdens.

"If it were not for the things that go wrong in your work, for the difficult people you have to deal with, for the burden of the decisions you have to make, and for the responsibility you carry, a lesser person could do your job at about half of what you make."

— *Nido R. Quebein*
From his powerful book,
How to Get Anything You Want!

"Warfare constantly requires adaptation and innovation."

— *Richard Danzig,*
Secretary to the Navy

He's right, but this is also true of business warfare!

Declare war on your competitors!

Why most of your competitors are EASY to beat:

Most small business people are not focused on the few projects that can make them the most money. They have no real game plan. Some of the most ambitious ones are very busy — but are not focused. Because of this, they are easy to beat! All you have to do is stay focused on the small number of projects that have the ability to make you the largest amount of money in the fastest time! *Remember, it's more important to do the right things than to do things right.*

The 3 "F's" of selling to their emotions.
Know your prospects' BIGGEST...

☞ **Fears**,

☞ **Frustrations**,

and

☞ **Failures!**

Let that question burn into your brain. Spend some time thinking about it very carefully. Then start building your sales message around these key areas. Don't pussyfoot around these areas. Clearly bring all of them up and show and tell your prospective buyers how you will solve each one of these things for them.

NEVER abdicate your marketing.

Your marketing (all the specific things you do to attract and retain customers and do the maximum amount of repeat business with them for the largest profit) is much too important to turn over to someone else.

There are so many consultants and freelancers who want you to "let them do it all for you." *Don't do it!*

⚜ GOYA! ⚜

Action generates inspiration! The way to get more great ideas is move! You gotta get off your ass every day and start working on the projects that stand the greatest chance of making you the LARGEST amount of money.

It seems simple and it is simple. Yet, how many people do this religiously?

What is your #1 competitive advantage?

You must be able to answer this question in the clearest way... *and it has to be a great answer!* Aristotle Onassis said, "The secret to business is to know something that none of your competitors know."

→ *Shipped to You for No Cost or Obligation!* Go to: www.PTIW.com/FreeBook

Bill Glazer's... Info-Marketing Formula:

1. Quality product.
2. Quality lead.
3. Marketing funnel (sequential follow-up mailings).
4. Risk reversal.
5. Continuity income.
6. What's next?

This simple six-step formula can make you massive sums of money! *It's a proven millionaire-maker!*

The best marketing ideas from one industry are easily *transferable* to your market.

Stay open! Think! *Be creative!* The more you do to expand your awareness of the fact that ideas are transferable — the better. You will be able to find all the ways you can add and combine the best ideas that other markets are using.

Most of your competitors are LOCKED into their own little world. They're about as creative as a head of cabbage! This makes it easy for you to step in, do something BOLD and new, and dominate your market!

ஐఆ

Change is the only thing that is permanent.

ஐఆ

One good golf shot wipes out a hundred bad ones!

Keep playing for that one good shot.

Why prospects DON'T buy right away:

1. Not enough pain with their current situation.
2. They don't perceive they have a need.
3. They can't distinguish that you're any better.
4. They don't trust you, your company, or your offer.
5. They don't trust themselves or think it will work for them.
6. You did not follow-up enough or put enough pressure on them.

Notice how "not having the money" is not on the list?

Thinking your entire marketing plan out from every angle — on paper — is a form of action.

Your best ideas will come to you while you are in the process of figuring everything out on paper. Setting your financial goals, working out projections, thinking through all of the potential challenges, and developing specific strategies to overcome the challenges.

Does all this sound like work? It's not. It's a game! The more you play the game — the more power you'll have!

When people pay — they pay attention!
Eric J. Bechtold

A good direct mail package is not afraid of the word NO!

➜ *Shipped to You for No Cost or Obligation! Go to: www.PTIW.com/FreeBook*

Do you own a business or the worst job in the world? Take this test to find out!

🔳🔳🔳

Can the business survive and even thrive <u>without</u> you?

🔳🔳🔳

It is to the degree that you can honestly say "YES!" to this question that will determine whether you in fact own a business or just a highly paid job.

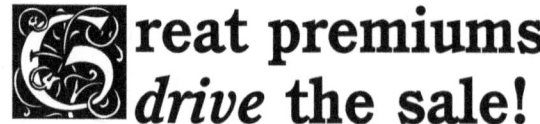reat premiums *drive* the sale!

Make your bonuses so attractive and sound so valuable that people are willing to buy your product or service <u>just</u> <u>to</u> <u>get</u> <u>the</u> <u>bonuses</u>.

The power of ROI!

It doesn't matter how much something costs. The only thing you should care about is how much <u>money</u> <u>it</u> <u>makes</u> <u>you</u>.

top looking for an easier and softer way.

Remember, all progress comes from discontent, not complacency. *Stay hungry* and <u>always</u> <u>let</u> <u>your</u> <u>reach</u> <u>exceed</u> <u>your</u> <u>grasp</u>!

$$$
Start charging more money for your stuff!

Someone has to be the <u>highest price</u> competitor... it might as well be you!

Charging more money lets you deliver higher quality products and services that attract the very best prospects in your market.

$$$

❦Learn by doing.❦

You can't let a simple thing like the fact that you've <u>never</u> done something or don't know how to do it stop you from doing it.

The fact that entrepreneurs are willing to boldly step out and face the unknown — and figure it all out as they go — is the one thing that separates them from everyone else.

Any fool can create and sell products, but it takes a true genius to create an ever-growing base of loyal fanatics who re-buy an increasing amount of products and services on a *frequent* basis.

ONE WAY is the <u>wrong way.</u>

More choices and options is the <u>right</u> way. Variety is power! *Flexibility is strength.*

→ *Shipped to You for No Cost or Obligation!* Go to: www.PTIW.com/FreeBook

$ $ $ $ $
The more HONEST and OPEN you are with your customers, the more BONDED they will be to you and the more they'll buy!

People are sick and tired of all the phony-sounding B.S. out there. THEY DON'T TRUST ANYONE ANYMORE. They are looking for something "REAL" and want to have a relationship with you. The more you do to tell them your carefully crafted "personal and private" details, the more money you'll make.

Try this and prove it to yourself!

$ $ $ $ $

"The Rambo types are the first to go."

Commanding Officer of SEALS Training at the Naval Special Warfare Center

The secret to survival in war or business is to be flexible and adaptable. There is no one way. You must have opposing skills and qualities that let you bend <u>without</u> breaking... You need qualities that let you take some of the most brutal beatings without smashing into a thousand pieces.

Success is a moving target.

You have to keep chasing it!

What are your <u>top 3 competitive advantages</u> and how can you exploit them in a bigger and better way?

Ask yourself this question, often.

Stop worrying about the cost of your leads!

I used to hang around with a group of marketers who sat around and bragged about the "low cost of leads." Each guy in the group would try to show off and give a lower number than the next guy.

BUT I <u>NEVER</u> PARTICIPATED IN THOSE CONVERSATIONS.

Why? Because the cost of the lead is no big deal! The only thing that matters is how much money you make! Sometimes your best bet is to spend more money on a lead than any of your other competitors are willing to spend. After all, the profitable conversion of the leads you generate is definitely <u>the</u> <u>most</u> <u>important</u> <u>thing</u>.

The lonely crowd.

People are "starving" for a little genuine and sincere recognition. Feed it to them and you'll get super rich!

Want proof from 2 people who knew?

"The two things people want more than sex or money are praise and recognition."

— *Mary Kay Ash*

"My life changed forever the day I realized that a man would die for a blue ribbon."

— *Napoleon Bonaparte*

Without duty... life is soft and boneless.

"I slept and dreamt that life was joy. I awoke and saw that life was duty. I acted and beheld that duty was joy."

— *Rabindranath Tagore*

Strive to be <u>more</u> "human" in all of your communications.

✓ Be real!

✓ Be raw!

✓ Be imperfect!

Let them feel what you feel and see the REAL person behind the words they are reading.

➔ *Shipped to You for No Cost or Obligation! Go to:* <u>www.PTIW.com/FreeBook</u>

Use the carrot and the stick to get them to buy from you!

Let the twin forces of <u>positive</u> and <u>negative</u> go to work for you.

Remember, people are more likely to act to avoid pain than to move towards pleasure. So give them something to move towards, but also to move away from. *Make them feel <u>both</u> good about buying and bad about not buying.*

Surround yourself with the best and brightest your money will buy!

When you hire people who are smarter than you are, you prove that you are smarter than they are!

The smartest and most capable people are always working for someone else. *They might as well be working for you!*

What is the #1 financial goal for your business <u>RIGHT NOW</u>?

You <u>must</u> have a clear target! A goal that excites you and causes you to stretch and reach for more!

"You <u>can't</u> kill an elephant with a BB gun!"
— *Bill Glazer*

People are trying to get HUGE results with a small amount of effort and expense.

YOU <u>CAN'T</u> DO IT!

So much of the slick, polished, and "professional looking" sales material is also the first to hit the trash can!

The marketplace is cluttered with all of this homogenized sales material. In an attempt to make it "perfect" it also comes off as being mass-produced and phony! *There is no edge to it... No personality... Nothing to suggest that a real, living, breathing person actually created it.*

Rock star or brain surgeon?

Your time is the most precious commodity you have. *So why would you want to sell it for any amount of money?* Don't do this! Find as many ways as you can to make money that have little or even nothing to do with the amount of time you put into it.

All great entrepreneurs are non-conformists because conformity leads to conventional results.

Conformists are people who follow the follower. Entrepreneurs are rule breakers who pave their own path.

Make yourself and/or your company so *unique* that you completely separate yourself from all of your competitors.

Get the prospects to seek you out!

→ *Shipped to You for No Cost or Obligation! Go to:* www.PTIW.com/FreeBook

What are the BRUTAL realities of your market that you have not been facing up to?

And what are you going to do about it?

The scam of "Lifetime Customer Value:"

➤ Many marketing professionals want you to focus on your "Lifetime Customer Value" so you won't think about the terrible response rates you're getting from the promotions they are putting together for you or helping you with.

➤ It's nice to focus on big-picture concepts such as lifetime value of your customers. But too much focus on this principle will definitely lead to bankruptcy!

➤ You #1 goal should always be getting the largest and fastest return on every dollar you spend on marketing. Once you do that — you can think of bigger picture issues.

Price resistance usually only lives in the business owner's mind.

The biggest obstacle to raising price is in the business owner's mind.

Become a ◆◆◆◆ marketing pitbull!

Most marketers give up on their prospective buyers way too soon. Don't do this! Be more relentless in all of your marketing efforts. Go after them in the most aggressive way — and stay after them.

Don't be too cheap when it comes to buying customers.

- ✓ Every customer <u>must</u> <u>be</u> <u>bought</u>... but most marketers are trying to do this as cheaply as possible.
- ✓ New customer acquisition is an investment towards future profits. This is one area of your marketing where you really need to be consistently BOLD!
- ✓ All of your profits come from doing more business with your current customers, but new customers are still the life-blood of your business! <u>You must build the most aggressive marketing system possible</u> — that can consistently bring you the largest number of new customers. Do all this right and you will have a powerful marketing advantage over your competitors.
- ✓ So what is an aggressive new customer acquisition program? Simple. Often it means losing some money on the initial sale. This scares most people and can be very risky, but it can also produce great rewards!

⊱Screw fear!⊰

Fear is the enemy of all success. It can have some positive benefits (fear of bankruptcy or prison!), but most of the time all it does is hold people back and stop them from getting the best of everything that could and should be theirs.

Having thousands of powerful direct mail sales letters (and the follow-up sales material that goes out after you generate the leads) is like having a GIANT ARMY of the very best salespeople who <u>never complain</u>... <u>always deliver</u> their best performance... and <u>never ask for a raise</u>!

❝I'm grateful to audiences for watching me and for enjoying what I do — but I'm not one of those who believe that a successful entertainer is made by the public, as is so often said. You become successful, the way I see it, only if you're good enough to deliver what the public enjoys. If you're not, you won't have any audience; so the performer really has more to do with his success than the public does.

Johnny Carson from a December 1967 Playboy Magazine Interview

<u>This is one of the most powerful marketing concepts you will ever learn and master.</u> The things that people want and need are usually the opposite of each other. So it's up to us marketers to create offers that contain the appearance of giving them what they really want, while also containing the things we know they need the most.

→ *Shipped to You for No Cost or Obligation!* Go to: www.PTIW.com/FreeBook

To the average prospect — there is <u>nothing</u> <u>more</u> <u>worthless</u> <u>than</u> <u>a</u> <u>sales</u> <u>pitch</u>. *Most people will go out of their way to avoid a salesman who is trying to sell them something.*

- → To the average prospect — salespeople are a dime a dozen. They are worthless.
- → Because of this, the last thing you should ever want is to be perceived as a salesperson.
- → What people do want and place great value on are celebrities and experts who command confidence. Once you create that position in their minds, you will have the attractor factor that draws them to you.

Develop educated-based marketing messages and strive to be known as a trusted adviser.

Everyone wants to do business with an expert. Re-invent yourself to be seen as the foremost expert in your area and they'll stand in line with money in hand.

PAIN is part of the process.

Embrace it...

Deal with it...

Even learn to enjoy it!

Wisdom from the founder of *Modern Advertising*:

"Ask a person to take a chance on you, and you have a fight. Offer to take a chance on him, and the way is easy.

I have always taken chances on the other fellow. I have analyzed my proposition until I made sure that he had <u>the</u> <u>best</u> <u>end</u> of the bargain. Then I had something that people could not well neglect.

I have been robbed plenty, but the robbery cost me ten times less than trying to enforce any safe proposition."

— *Claude Hopkins*
(On why giving away free samples and taking other actions to <u>invest</u> <u>in</u> <u>the</u> <u>prospect</u> <u>first</u>, before you ask for their money is so important.)

Good judgment comes from experience — and experience comes from bad judgment.

Make more mistakes... faster... and learn from them.

The REAL breakfast of champions is not Wheaties cereal...

It's getting up early every morning while the rest of the world is still asleep and putting in 3 or 4 hours of the most intense and focused work!

Why don't more people do this?

<u>Simply this</u>: It's too painful! And yet, when you eat a little bit of this pain on a daily basis, you grow very strong!

What you sell must appear to be very hard to get — but super easy to buy!

- The more you can do to create the illusion that what you have to offer would be extremely difficult for them to get without you, your company, and/or whatever you offer — the better.
- Build your case! Prove to them that what you have is extremely difficult and very hard or even impossible to get on their own. Apply the pressure... Make them see and feel it! Then and only then should you make it very easy for them to buy.

Give away a small piece of the LARGER THING you want to ultimately sell to them.

∞

Give away your <u>BEST STUFF</u> — then upsell the hell out of them!

→ *Shipped to You for No Cost or Obligation!* Go to: www.PTIW.com/FreeBook

You are only looking for the few who "can" and "will" — rather than the larger number who "can't" and "won't."

The power of the intangible.

★ Master salespeople <u>always</u> focus on selling the intangible aspects of our products or services. This takes a greater degree of skill — but the increase in revenue can be huge!

★ The intangible aspects of many products and services is where the real money is to be made. The dream will <u>always</u> transcend the reality. So sell the dream! The hope! The promise! Paint the picture BIG... and BRIGHT!

★ Never be afraid to over-hype your offers. Turn up the volume full blast. The minute you think you have gone too far means you probably still have a ways to go.

Why we <u>don't</u> get the sales conversions we want:

1) Prospect is not qualified enough.
   — This is the #1 problem. The rest of the items on the list are not prioritized.
2) There is not a good enough reason to cause them to buy now!
3) The back-end offer is not related closely enough to your initial sale.
4) You tried to move them too far too fast.
   — In other words, you asked new prospects and/or very skeptical customers to give you too much money, too quickly.
5) There was no "irresistible" offer.
6) You gave up on them too soon!
   — In other words, you did not do enough follow-up marketing.
7) Poor salesmanship!
   — You simply did a lousy job of selling them — and did not do enough to prove to them that what you had to offer was worth far more than the money you were asking for in exchange.

That's it!

"When I'm one of 'them' I have credibility."

— *David Lupberger*

One of the BIGGEST CHALLENGES in business today is eliminating all of the distractions and interruptions that drain us of our energy and keep us from focusing.

The two enemies of the entrepreneurial life:

🦋 PEACE and COMFORT. 🦋

➤ Entrepreneurs thrive under pressure! We need new challenges. New obstacles. New problems to solve. These things spur us into action and it is through the actions we take that everything great is achieved.

➤ You must remain disturbed! Stay angry and restless! Embrace all of the problems — frustrations — and confusion! Let the pain of these seemingly negative situations drive you forward!

➤ The thing I hate most is when somebody tells me to "take it easy." I hate that! If they keep doing this I will finally get in their face and scream, "I'll take it easy when I'm dead!"

EMOTIONAL EMPOWERMENT

The negative emotions are a vital part of our human nature. Stop suppressing them — and start re-focusing them. They contain a tremendous amount of energy — <u>if you use them correctly</u>. Like fire, they can burn down your house (with you inside) or they can keep you alive on the coldest winter day. Your choice. But when you suppress them — you lose all of the amazing energy they contain to keep you in the game.

ANGER = Determination.

GREED = Ambition.

LUST = Machismo.

FEAR = Caution and power.

ENVY = Positive revenge.

HATE = Competitive power.

FEAR (also) = Amazing bursts of energy and excitement!

Gary Halbert used to say:

"You'll always achieve more through movement than meditation."

It never ceases to amaze me at the way the ideas flow to me after I get through an extremely difficult project that caused me so much pain and confusion. Getting past that short-term nightmare is like blowing up the dam!

You must become and remain your #1 fan!

Business can be a sad and lonely trip. You must continue to believe in yourself when nobody else does. This will empower you to keep getting back up every time you get knocked down.

Take your business to the next level.

- How can you serve it up even <u>better</u> than everyone else?
- What are the BIGGEST PROBLEMS in your market that none of your competitors are solving? *How can you solve them?*
- Look for problems in your market. Talk with your best customers and prospects.

Pain, problems, challenges, obstacles, heartbreak, disappointment, and setbacks are good!

In fact, you must have more of them!

Adversity of all kinds contains raw emotional power that you can use to fuel your inner fire! The key is to remind yourself of this — as you are in the middle of it all. During those times, you must SLAP YOURSELF IN THE FACE and <u>snap out of it</u>!

Let them spur you on to the right actions!

Wealth-making wisdom from an oil tycoon who knew:

"The more wells you drill, the greater chance you have of finding oil."

— *H.L. Hunt*

Fast was never fast enough for H.L. Hunt. "Drill, drill, drill!" was his company's mantra.

So what? Who cares? What's in it for me?

These are three things that people are unconsciously thinking as they're reading your copy or listening to your sales pitch.

As you are editing your material, you should go over it with the same 3 questions in your head. Then cut <u>anything</u> that doesn't answer those questions in the clearest and boldest way.

"Remember, we are dealing with people who are unpredictable. What they demand one year they may disdain the next."

— *Emma Bailey (1962)*

◈ She goes on to say, "Something which brought high prices five years ago may go begging now!"

◈ Emma wrote this in 1962, but it's <u>even</u> *more* <u>true</u> in today's crazy world of heavy competition and instant result-seeking prospects.

◈ Promotions that brought in a ton of profits last quarter may totally bomb a few short months later!

Research is what you are doing when <u>you</u> <u>don't</u> <u>know</u> what you're doing!

Your level of <u>success</u> is determined by your *ability* and *capacity* to handle large amounts of uncertainty.

→ *Shipped to You for No Cost or Obligation!* Go to: www.PTIW.com/FreeBook

Outrageous marketing tip:

➤ *"When in doubt, make a fool of yourself. There is a microscopically thin line between being brilliantly creative and acting like the most gigantic idiot on earth. So what the hell, leap!"*
— *Cynthia Heimel*

➤ Cynthia is right! Most of us are way too afraid to push the envelope. We hold back. We fear going over the top — but our marketing messages are as boring as mud.

➤ There really is a thin line between being brilliantly creative and acting like a complete idiot!

Upsell strategy: The best time to get someone to say "YES!" to you is right after they say "YES!" to you about something else!

✓ This is the single greatest time they are the most open and receptive to doing whatever you want them to do. Their checkbook is open and they're handing you the pen!

The bottom line speaks the *loudest!*

A friendship built around the business is a hell of a lot better than a business that's built around a friendship.

(The former can work — while the latter seldom does.)

The CREATIVE BLOWOUT!

The creative mind feeds off variety! It can be a little crazy at times (or all the time!), but you must have many projects going at the same time. Be willing to suffer through the pain of being overwhelmed, frustrated, and confused. *It's okay to feel these things!* No matter how bad it feels, nobody ever died from the intense pain of confusion or frustration!

RISK is the price you pay for *opportunity*.

❝The beauty of this is its simplicity. If the plan gets too complex something always goes wrong.❞

— *Walter (John Goodman) in "The Big Lebowski"*

It's good to be rich!

"He that is without money may as well be buried in a rice tub, with his mouth sewn shut."

— *Chinese Proverb*

Can you be any more graphic than being buried in a rice tub with your mouth sewn shut? No! And to think this was written many hundreds of years ago!

→ *Shipped to You for No Cost or Obligation!* Go to: www.PTIW.com/FreeBook

CREATIVITY and BUSINESS.

- Most people would never think of business as a creative pursuit. And most businesses aren't! In fact, most businesses are as boring as mud!
- But a few visionary entrepreneurs continue to show us that it does not have to be this way. These people make business fun and exciting for all of their customers.

◊◊◊◊◊◊◊◊◊◊◊◊◊

Let the **numbers** tell you what to do.

◊◊◊◊◊◊◊◊◊◊◊◊◊

Winning isn't everything... but losing REALLY SUCKS!

A great Dorothea Brande quote from her 1936 book, "Wake Up and Live!":

"Usually, far from overrating our abilities, we do not understand how great they are. The reason for this underestimation of ourselves will be considered later, but it is well to realize that few except the truly insane believe themselves suited for careers far beyond their full powers."

Do you have to be crazy to succeed in the biggest possible way? <u>Maybe!</u> So go crazy! Set goals that are higher than anything you can imagine. Who knows, you might just grow into them.

Or in an outrageous attempt to achieve these goals, you could set off in a whole new direction you would have never imagined had you not decided to THINK and ACT bigger.

Wisdom from New York's BIGGEST thinker

*— Donald Trump
from The Art of the Deal:*

"People think I'm a gambler. I've never gambled in my life. To me, a gambler is someone who plays slot machines. I prefer to own slot machines! It's a good business being the house... If you go for a home run on every pitch, you're going to strike out a lot. I try never to leave myself too exposed, even if it means sometimes settling for a triple, a double, or even, on rare occasions, a single."

A major part of all success can simply be boiled down to the willingness to do what everyone around you is unwilling or unable to do.

If you're looking for a secret you can fit on a 3" x 5" index card — THERE IT IS!

Most entrepreneurs don't think BIG enough... They waste $1,000 worth of time and energy on a $100 problem.

> ➤ *Don't do this!* Keep your eye on the prize! Be willing to walk over many $100.00 bills to get to the millions!

What about love and money?

When I look at the times I made the most money in the shortest periods of time, it was when I was totally in love with what I was doing. This is the money making power nobody talks about. You must fall passionately in love with your business or at least the parts of it that bring you the most money. ***Love is power!*** You are most alive when you're in love and — because of this — you will find a way to do amazing things that you couldn't begin to ever do without this awesome invisible power.

➔ *Shipped to You for No Cost or Obligation!* Go to: www.PTIW.com/FreeBook

Most advertising <u>sucks</u>!

"The advertising business is going down the drain. It's being pulled down by the people who create it, who don't know how to sell anything, who have never sold anything in their lives... who despise selling, whose mission in life is to be clever show-offs and con clients into giving them money to display originality and genius."

— *David Ogilvy*

The experience of taking something from your head, putting it on paper, sending it out, and then bringing in millions of dollars has to be one of the greatest feelings on earth!

Talk about the power of manifestation. Wow!
This is alchemy in action!

Let this be your guiding mantra:

"Your job is to go as far as you can see. You will then see far enough to go further."

— *Brian Tracy*

The single greatest quality of the entrepreneur is the courage to dream BIG dreams and dare to move forward — with only the haziest idea of how it's all going to come together!

Educational marketing is the best way to deliver any sales message because:

1. It lets the best prospective buyers seek you out.

2. It empowers those buyers by making it appear as if it were <u>their</u> <u>choice</u> to come to you.

3. It lowers their sales resistance and lets them "sell themselves" on you, your company, or your products and services.

4. It makes people want to do business with you! They come to you ready, willing, and able to pay the premium prices you charge.

In short, this form of marketing makes the best prospective buyers in your market think and feel that it is <u>their</u> <u>choice</u> to do business with you. *They come to you already sold!*

Success leaves clues and when you study the lives of all super-successful people — you will discover that they never did it by themselves. **There was always a group of people behind and sometimes in front of them — every step of the way.**

It's the unique combination of the talents, skills, experience, support, and guidance of all of those people that made the biggest difference. Without these people — and everything they brought to the table — the "superstar" at the top would have never made it. *Or at least they would have never made it on such a grand scale.*

Answers come from action!

Want more answers? *Take more action!* In fact, you must take MASSIVE ACTION! Move in a thousand directions! Test a million things as fast as you can. *Move damn it, move!*

The killer disease of the 21st Century:

"Information OVERLOAD!"

People are absolutely positively OVERWHELMED with too much information... and they can't take one more idea or sales pitch! Many salespeople and marketers confuse information with communication. They try to tell them too much, too fast, and it's all information that means something to the marketer but it's not necessarily perceived as IMPORTANT to the prospect.

Start buying more stuff...
◆RIGHT NOW!◆

The more stuff you buy — the more money you can make! I'm serious. This is not a joke. If you truly want to crawl inside of the minds and hearts of your average prospective buyer — you must continue to buy the same stuff that he or she is buying! Or at least buy as many things as possible (via direct response marketing) from an ultra-competitive marketplace where each company must chase after you!

When you buy a lot of stuff from the market you sell to – or an active marketplace that you are very interested in – you re-experience the RUSH and the THRILL of buying! You begin to remember how it feels to be a rabid buyer! Or if you never have been a rabid buyer – you experience it for the first time. This is an important key to fully understanding the emotional side of the marketing process. By doing this, you begin to put yourself into the shoes of the people you sell to. Buy enough stuff and you will (hopefully) become a rabid buyer yourself! *This will make you a much better marketer!*

→ *Shipped to You for No Cost or Obligation!* Go to: www.PTIW.com/FreeBook

The best marketers are always the ones who are the most relentless in their follow-up activities. Once they attract a highly qualified prospect, they <u>don't</u> give up! They stay after them. They bug the hell out of them. **They try to do anything and everything they can to get the sale!**

<u>BOTTOM LINE</u>: Most marketers give up way too soon. And because of it, they leave a lot of money on the table that could and should be theirs.

A good headline will always answer the question: "What's in it for me?"

Go back and read your headlines and body copy with the attitude of "So what?" or "Who cares?" Be as apathetic or skeptical as you possibly can. Then make changes accordingly.

"The potential problem is always the same: Can you sell it, and at what price for how long?"

— *Paul MacAvoy,*
Yale Economics Professor

This quote jumped off the page because I've never heard such simple words that were more true from a college professor! <u>I was shocked</u>! It seems so simple, and yet all entrepreneurs suffer from the fact that we fall in love with what we are doing and are blinded by our passion. We tend to suffer from the delusion that just because we love something — then so will many other people.

<u>Mantra of the visionary leader:</u>

"If I'd asked people what they wanted, they would have asked for a better horse."

— *Henry Ford*

This whole idea that we must "ask the customer what they want and listen closely" is a load of crap! People buy in an emotional vacuum. The only way to know what they really want is to test a lot of different things and then watch the numbers closely. Then develop new products and services around the things they bought the most (while continuing to test and track the results).

From master marketing guru Russ von Hoelscher:

"Whatever tugs at their heart also tugs at their wallet!"

Russ said these words to me when we were talking about the importance of coming up with a great emotional story behind every offer you make. The more real, raw, and true this story is — *the more money you will make!*

A good metaphor is a shortcut to instant understanding.

- Mastering the art of metaphors will help you sell more stuff to more people. This is your ultimate tool for making complicated things very simple.
- The key is to find the most powerful comparisons that your prospect can relate to.

A big fat lie that you have bought into.

A lot of businesspeople have bought into the idea that stress is bad or dangerous... But that is a lie! Yes, we have all been lied to and didn't even know it. Stress is a good and necessary thing. It's strain that kills — not stress (remember that). This is important because you must push yourself harder! The stress is a great thing! Just be sure you pull back... rest... and re-charge. Too much stress without plenty of intervals of rest leads to strain.

So many people who believe that "stress is bad" never push themselves hard enough and never achieve the success that could be theirs.

This is brilliant!

When asked how he dealt with the 14 years of drought in his career when nobody was calling... and the parts he was being offered SUCKED...
John Travolta said, "I never stopped believing in myself — no matter what other people said about me or my future."

In fact, when I heard that John said this — I instantly recognized it as one of the most important qualities that all of the great entrepreneurs possess.

→ *Shipped to You for No Cost or Obligation! Go to: www.PTIW.com/FreeBook*

> "Advertising is what you do when you can't go see somebody. That's all it is."
> — *Fairfax Cane*

All we are doing is trying to the best of our ability to replace a live salesperson. We are using our sales materials and strategies to replace part or all of what a live salesperson does.

The days of trying to make money in direct-response marketing without using sales professionals — to follow-up and close sales — is over!

It is amazing to me that we were able to run our business without salespeople for so many years...

Even more amazing that others are still trying to make it without salespeople who follow up, close (with more pressure), and build the all-important personal relationships that make all of the upselling and re-selling so much faster, easier, and more profitable.

Obstacles are the things you see when you take your eyes off your goals.

- Stay focused!
- What are your primary goals that are most important to you? What are you doing TODAY to achieve those goals in the BIGGEST way?
- You must have a clear and compelling answer to that question.

One of my favorite quotes came from the transcripts of a speech that Ernest Holmes gave in the early 1900s:

> **"I used to think that other men were great — then I got off of my knees!"**

I read that quote — loved it — and tattooed it deep into my brain! And I realized this simple truth: it is wrong to place too much importance on anyone. See the greatness in certain qualities they have or in certain actions they take, but never think of them as great.

Do EVERYTHING you can to make sure you are a welcome guest instead of an annoying pest!

➢ Make it feel that <u>they</u> came to you instead of you going to them!

➢ People hate to be <u>sold</u> anything, but they love to <u>buy</u>!

➢ The key: *You must do all you can to make it feel as if it was their choice and not yours!*

The secret of success can be as simple as building your entire business around the ultimate lifestyle you most want to live.

Simple... but not easy. Of course, all of the most <u>fulfilling</u> things in life and business are also the ones that tend to be the most difficult (at least part of the time).

"THINKING BIG" has become a catchphrase for many entrepreneurs, but "THINKING BROAD" is something almost nobody talks about. It's <u>just</u> <u>as</u> <u>important</u> — if not more important.

What is thinking broadly all about?

Thinking broadly is all about trying to think things through from as many angles as possible, thinking conceptually, and looking at your business from the top down (instead of from the bottom up). You must see the "connections" that others can't see.

The key to making the largest amount of back-end profits is to OVER-DELIVER on your front-end fulfillment!

BLOW THEIR MIND! Make them say, "Holy crap! I can't believe they gave me so much stuff (or such a great deal)!" Then — when you offer them your back-end package — <u>they'll</u> <u>buy</u> <u>like</u> <u>crazy</u>!

One of the keys to becoming a great marketer is to put as much distance as you can between yourself and the day-to-day grind of your business.

- Hire the most competent people you can find to run your day-to-day operations. Treat them well (including pay) and then let them take care of this vital but boring and energy-zapping part of your business.
- Then, think of your company as if it were a product on a shelf and market it accordingly.

Power perceived is power achieved!

Enter the room like you own the place! Always hold your head high and confidently demand that they give you their money!

Facts can hide the truth.

And they can tell almost any story you want to tell.

You'll never do great things by focusing on your limitations.

Instead, you must channel all of your energy into the possibilities.

"Everything you want is on the other side of your comfort zone."

— *Ted Ciuba*

You can't cost-cut your way to prosperity.

➢ Many business owners spend way too much time focusing on cutting expenses. The problem: Whatever you focus on expands! The more expenses they cut — the more they want to cut. Then they keep cutting back <u>until</u> <u>they</u> <u>don't</u> <u>have</u> <u>a</u> <u>business</u> <u>anymore</u>!

➢ Your main focus must ALWAYS be on increasing your sales and profits. Think offensively 70% of the time and defensively the other 30%. This will keep your focus where it must be to build your business and keep it super profitable.

<u>Marketing</u>: The attracting and retaining of the very best prospective buyers for maximum profitability is a process and never an event.

You learn... grow... adapt... and roll with the changes.

The tiger fails to catch his prey 95% of the time...

And yet <u>lives</u> <u>like</u> <u>a</u> <u>king</u> on the 5% he does catch!

➜ *Shipped to You for No Cost or Obligation!* Go to: www.PTIW.com/FreeBook

❝You're never going to be a really good professional speaker until you've been in a number of really bad speaking situations.**❞**
— *Jim Cathcart*

- When it comes to your own personal development — it's the hard times that count the most. The good times are not that good. You must willingly put yourself through as many "<u>BAD</u>" situations as possible... to develop your skills. You gotta walk through the fire!

- Very few people actually enjoy the most difficult periods... and yet these are the times of the greatest growth. Working through these terrible times makes you stronger and wiser. It is the secret to developing yourself in the fullest way.

෩෬ The secret to staying young:

You don't stop playing because you grow old... You grow old because you stopped playing. SO <u>NEVER</u> STOP!
෩෬

Work in spurts!

One of the secrets to my own high level of productivity is the simple, but powerful, fact that I do most of my work in short bursts of high intensity!

I catch myself on fire... and then I burn brightly for these brief periods. The larger projects become strings of as many of these smaller pieces that are stitched together.

Make your business a game that you play — *and then play to win!*

<u>This is much more than some silly bumper sticker idea</u>! This is a major success principle that makes you more money and lets you get more joy and satisfaction out of your business. It also makes it easier to deal with all of the adversity that hits you on a daily... weekly... monthly... and yearly basis. When you're playing a game to win — <u>you are a contender</u>! The entire purpose and meaning for why you do what you do is so much different than someone who is "trying to make a lot of money." Can you see this? I hope so!

MORE is better!

<u>Want to achieve more?</u>
Then do more! It's that simple.
Massive action is the key.
You must <u>always</u> do much more
than you think you have to do
in order to reach your goals.
Remember that. It <u>always</u>
takes more — not less —
at least in the beginning.

Mark Victor Hansen said he got rejected 144 different times before a publisher said "<u>YES!</u>" to the first *Chicken Soup for the Soul* books. <u>Now they've sold more than 100 million books</u>!

Imagine all the jealous people who say that Mark and his business partner, Jack Canfield, got lucky.

There is <u>no such thing</u> as time management!

◈ Time is like the weather... it cannot be managed or controlled. It is what it is. You have ZERO power over it.

◈ Because of this, the whole concept of "time management" is misleading and weak.

◈ A much better concept is "action management." The reason is simple: *You can control your actions!* What you decide to do at any given moment is largely within your control. And there are many things you can do to take BETTER actions that produce more of the results you want.

❝Our life is frittered away by detail... Simplify, simplify, simplify! Simplicity of life and the elevation of purpose.❞
— *Henry David Thoreau*

> How many things can you live without?
> What is <u>really</u> important and what's not?
> The fewer things you want — the simpler your life and business will be.

→ *Shipped to You for No Cost or Obligation!* Go to: <u>www.PTIW.com/FreeBook</u>

It's NEVER about the money.

The highest-qualified prospects <u>almost</u> <u>never</u> think about price… and when they do it's at the bottom of their list of priorities.

Most sales are lost over objections that the prospect never tells you about. They simply don't have enough confidence that your product or service is the right one for them. If it is more expensive — they are not convinced that the added advantages they will get are worth the extra money you are charging. *It's up to you to convince them!*

$$$$$$

People will always do things for THEIR reasons — never <u>YOURS</u>!

Forget about yourself and only care about and/or communicate the things that are most important to them.

$$$$$$

Diversity leads to stability.

Find <u>as</u> <u>many</u> <u>different</u> <u>ways</u> as you can to get the results you want.

MORE is better!

Find a business that can consume you!

- ◈ One that can fully captivate you.
- ◈ One that you can fall completely and totally in love with!
- ◈ One that will absorb you… challenge you… interest and excite you. These businesses are out there and if you can't find one – create one!

→CHARGE MORE!

Are people complaining that your prices are too high? If so — DON'T LOWER THEM — just sell harder!

The fact that your prices are too high is almost never the problem. If you get this objection too much, you must ask this question: "What are you doing to prove to people — beyond any doubt — that what you offer is worth FAR MORE than the money you're asking them to give you?"

It's up to you to build the value up by educating them in every way about why you charge premium prices.

Most salespeople are so busy selling — they do not give the prospect a chance to buy! **This is no joke:**

1. They do all the talking and no listening.
2. They never engage the prospective buyer.
3. They never do the kinds of things that build trust.
4. They never give the prospect the chance to feel like they want to feel: *The most important person on earth!*
5. They never get the prospect to reveal the real reasons they're not buying.

It's all about the ego of the salesperson and NEVER about helping the prospect get what they want the most.

Know your limitations.

Do you?
Compensate for them in as many ways as possible.

Making a lot of money is NOT about doing what you love.

It's about finding out what produces the biggest results and choosing to fall in love with those things.

→ *Shipped to You for No Cost or Obligation! Go to: www.PTIW.com/FreeBook*

Create advertising that does not look and feel like advertising.

- Make it look like public relations.
- Make it look like education.
- Make it look like one friend writing or communicating in some way to another friend.
- Make it all about them and how you can somehow give them more of what you <u>know</u> they want the most.
- Make it look hokey! And what is that? I'm glad you asked! Make it more fun and exciting for the people in your target market!

These are the kinds of things that will completely separate you from all of your competitors. You'll stand out... get noticed... wake the right people up... and get them involved. This of course leads them down the main path to spend more money more often in even larger amounts — while also advising all of their friends to do the same!

Leap without looking!

It's the entrepreneurial way.

THE <u>DICTATOR!</u>

The average customer is more demanding than ever!
More choices make them feel more empowered!

Persuasion is telling someone what to do WITHOUT actually telling them what to do!

- Nobody wants to be told what to do... So our job is to get them to do what we want them to do without actually telling them!
- We do <u>everything</u> <u>possible</u> to make them feel as if they are coming to us rather than us going to them.
- We make them feel as if they are the ones who are in power.
- We let them feel as if they are buying rather than us selling.
- We let them feel that spending their money with us is definitely in their best self-interest.

110 FREE 30-Page Book "Get Paid Every Time Our Phone Rings!" →

Throw away all of your books on leadership. I can give all of it to you in 3 very simple words:

Take total responsibility.

Sound too simple? It's not. Don't let the simplicity fool you. There is nothing more difficult than taking complete and total responsibility for everything that happens in your life and business. *It is the hardest thing you will ever do.* There is so much you cannot control and yet you must still assume total responsibility for all of your *actions* and *reactions*.

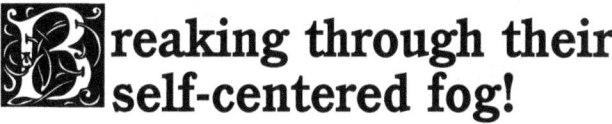
Breaking through their self-centered fog!

All people have a very thick layer of self-centeredness that shields and protects them. Your offer is like the warm sun that penetrates the self-centered fog of the prospective buyer!

The problem is, the prospective buyers are moving so fast that you only have a very short amount of time for the heat of the offer to burn through their fog. You must do it fast! *What's the fastest way to do it?* Do whatever it takes to make your offer personal to them. It must speak to them in the most compelling and direct way possible or won't have time to breakthrough.

Are you focused on the obstacles *or the objectives?*

Both are important, but putting more focus on the latter will always make you more money.

One great golf shot wipes out a hundred bad ones.

➔ *Shipped to You for No Cost or Obligation!* Go to: www.PTIW.com/FreeBook

Stay hungry!

Kids ask an average of 120 questions a day.

They are hungry!
They're curious!
They have a very powerful need to know!
Their filters are wide open!

But how many questions does the <u>average</u> adult ask? SIX!!! YES, from 120 questions a day to 6!

Is it any wonder why most adults are about as creative as a head of lettuce?

How to double or triple your entire business... in <u>ONE</u> <u>EASY</u> <u>STEP</u>!

Just get each of your best customers to refer one other person to you who also ends up becoming a good customer and you have doubled your entire business! Get them to each refer two and your business is now 3 TIMES BIGGER and so much more profitable!

It's so simple, isn't it? YES! Of course, it's not easy — but <u>you</u> <u>can</u> <u>do</u> <u>it</u> with the right referral program that greatly rewards your customers for giving you the names and addresses (and their own endorsement) of a handful of other people they personally know and believe could greatly benefit from what you sell.

People only notice the birds with the brightest colors!

✦✦✦

What are you doing to get the right people to <u>notice</u> <u>you</u>?

Become enlightened... ◘ LIGHTEN UP! ◘

See your life and business through the eyes of a great comedy genius. Your most creative ideas will only come to you when you are totally fired up! You can't be too serious... *Do whatever it takes, each day, to lighten up!*

What do you say when you've already said everything you have to say a million times?

Answer: Say it 1,000,001 times!

Lesson: The customers will NEVER get tired of hearing good sales pitch stories that excite them and offer them something they badly want. Just because you're sick and tired of telling these sales stories to them does not mean that they are tired of hearing them.

Are you cheating?

- People laugh when I tell them that I write the same sales letter over and over again. They think it's a joke. And once they realize that I'm not joking — they think I'm doing something wrong! I'm not. All I am doing is being creative!
- *There is nothing worse than the blank screen or page!* Having very good models that you can take ideas from is the fun and creative part of producing sales material that sells!
- This is a MAJOR shortcut! It is a faster and easier way to write the very best sales letters you can possibly write. You'll get a greater abundance of powerful selling ideas you can work with — and if you start with the best models — those ideas will be much more powerful.
- Creating new sales material from a pile of existing material is what creativity is all about!

Success comes from self-discipline.

So does real self-esteem! Those who want more self-esteem must do more esteemable activities more often! It's as simple as that. Self-discipline is all about forcing yourself to do the most important things you know you must do (but often don't feel like doing).

If you do what everyone else is doing — you're going to get the results that everyone else is getting... which are average, at best.

If you want extraordinary results you MUST do extraordinary things!

→ *Shipped to You for No Cost or Obligation!* Go to: www.PTIW.com/FreeBook

The ugly truth...

➤ Even the most honest people — with the highest of all integrity — still think it's okay to lie to a salesperson.

THOUGHT JOGGERS:

→ What are your top five greatest selling messages?

→ Why should they buy from <u>YOU</u> and not someone else?

→ What are the strongest inducements that will make them buy right now?
- *The best offer?*
- *The best bribe?*

→ What is the <u>strongest</u> and <u>most</u> <u>believable</u> reason to get them to send you their money right away?

The Killer Marketer:

We smell blood every time one of our promotions works... And we only want more!

How To Create Your Marketing System:

1. You find out what works best (through testing).

2. Then you expand those activities as far as possible. You do more testing to discover "<u>how high is high?</u>"

3. Then you <u>focus</u> on the areas that bring you the best results. You create procedures that do those things automatically.

Most managers...
are not demanding enough from their people and holding them accountable. This is especially true with huge companies.

Someone once told me the story of a wealthy land owner who called in one of his employees and said, "I've been reviewing the employee records and see you've been working here for 25 years to take care of our stables. Is that right?" The employee said, "YES!" And the owner replied, "But we sold all of our horses off 20 years ago. Isn't that correct?" And the employee said, "Yes, that's right, sir, and what would you like for me to do next?"

This may be a joke, but if you've been around business for a while, you instantly see the truth in this! *Most employees will do whatever you ask them to do – and nothing more.*

Making money and keeping it are <u>two</u> <u>entirely</u> <u>different</u> <u>things</u>.

Both require unique strategies.

Nine Essentials You Need to Know to Market Your Business.
by Misty Williams

Your chances for business success increase exponentially when you clearly understand the most important **essentials** for growing your business:

1. Know what you do best. 2. Know who your customers are. 3. Know how customers find you. 4. Know your "sales process." 5. Know where you add the most value. 6. Know your competitive business advantages. 7. Know where to spend your money. 8. Know the most painful and weakest areas of your business. 9. Know when to look for help.

*How can you improve in all nine of these vital areas?
Where is your strongest and weakest link?*

Great sales copy goes *straight* to the emotions!

- It's human warmth on paper!
- It's one-to-one personal communication.
- It's you and me sitting down face-to-face and having a warm heart-to-heart talk about a product or service that can truly help you.
- It must reek of sincerity.

→ *Shipped to You for No Cost or Obligation!* Go to: <u>www.PTIW.com/FreeBook</u>

◈ ◈ ◈
A closer's secret:
Have complete disregard for anything but the money!

◈ ◈ ◈

Only an entrepreneur can understand another entrepreneur.

Team dynamics from one of the world's greatest basketball coaches:

❝They said you have to use your five best players, but I found you win with the five who fit together the best.❞

— *Red Auerbach*
(9-Time NBA Champion as a Coach and 7-Time Champion as a General Manager)

You never get what you want — you only get what you expect!

High expectation is the key to taking your business to the next level.

A few words about consultants:

- It's <u>always</u> easy to give advice from a safe port.
- Just like it's <u>always</u> so much easier to take risks with someone else's money.

<u>Don't be scammed!</u>

Nobody has all the answers... no matter how good they may be at fooling people into believing so.

<u>Selling is a game!</u>

It's the game of understanding the people you sell to on the deepest level... Their biggest and most secret hopes, fears, and desires... And then using that knowledge to create the ultimate sales messages – that cut right to the heart – promising that you can give them what they want most.

> There is **so much joy** that comes from the long-term effects of a life of hard work, discipline, focus, goal setting, commitment, and daily striving to work towards your dream.

Getting old sucks! Except for one really cool thing:

Having the ability to reflect.

...It's a powerful thing!

It is great to have gained enough personal experiences to be able to look back and see things from your past that enable you to make the RIGHT CHOICES today.

→ FREE 30-Page Book at: www.PTIW.com/FreeBook

www.ingramcontent.com/pod-product-compliance
Lightning Source LLC
Chambersburg PA
CBHW081419160426
42813CB00087B/2617